PREACHING THE OLD TESTAMENT

PREACHING THE OLD TESTAMENT

Edited by
Scott M. Gibson

Foreword by
Haddon W. Robinson

BakerBooks
Grand Rapids, Michigan

Published by Baker Books
a division of Baker Publishing Group
P.O. Box 6287, Grand Rapids, MI 49516-6287
www.bakerbooks.com

Printed in the United States of America

Library of Congress Cataloging-in-Publication Data
Preaching the Old Testament / edited by Scott M. Gibson ; foreword by Haddon W. Robinson.
p. cm.
Includes bibliographical references.
ISBN 10: 0-8010-6623-9 (pbk.)
ISBN 978-0-8010-6623-8 (pbk.)
1. Bible. O.T.—Homiletical use. 2. Bible. O.T.—Sermons. 3. Preaching.
I. Gibson, Scott M., 1957–
BS1191.5.P74 2006
252—dc22 2006018860

In honor of
Walter C. Kaiser Jr.
preacher, professor, seminary president,
and
scholar

Contents

Acknowledgments

This book is a group effort. The contributors pulled together to produce an excellent collection of chapters designed to help preachers preach and at the same time honor Walter C. Kaiser Jr. I thank each author for his or her effort in making this book a reality.

Thanks also to Eric Dokken and David Hanke for their assistance in research and technical aid. In addition, I am grateful to the following people who gave insight into how preachers preach the Old Testament: Jeff Arthurs, Pat Batten, Keith Campbell, David Currie, Mark Debowski, Kent Edwards, Paul Hoffman, Conley Hughes, Jennie Martone, Glen Massey, Michael Mazzye, Charles Moore, Lisa Morrison, Bill Nicoson, Stephen Sebastian, Ken Shigematsu, Kevin Siscoe, Terry Smith, and Bryan Wilkerson.

Thanks, too, to the amazing Dianne Newhall. You are the best, Lady Di.

Thanks also to Barry H. Corey, vice president for education and academic dean at the South Hamilton campus of Gordon-Conwell Theological Seminary, for encouragement and support in the completion of this project.

A special word of thanks to Marge Kaiser for her help in gathering needed information for the book. I understand why Walt rises up and calls you blessed.

I am also blessed. I am grateful to the Lord for my wife, Rhonda, who continuously supports me with her love and encouragement. Again and again I affirm the words from the writer of Proverbs, who said, "He who finds a wife finds what is good and receives favor from the LORD" (Prov. 18:22). Thank you God for your favor.

Thank you to Baker Publishing Group, to Don Stephenson, Paul Brinkerhoff, Lindsey VanTuinen, Lauren Forsythe, and staff. You all are always so very helpful and kind—and patient, too! All that you do is appreciated.

This book is written in honor of Walter C. Kaiser Jr. Dr. Kaiser's career in education and preaching is stellar. His influence in the classroom, in the president and dean offices of two outstanding seminaries, and in the pulpit is recognized and esteemed by those in the evangelical community. This book is a small token of appreciation to him and to the Lord for this gifted servant. God has blessed us through you, Walt. Thank you and praise the Lord.

Foreword

Haddon W. Robinson

I have a good friend who is an Old Testament scholar. Several years ago, when his father turned eighty-five, the old gentleman determined that he would read through the Old Testament during the coming year for the first time. At the end of the year, the father testified, "I got through it, but I almost lost my faith!"

It would be pleasant to think that if the old man had attended a Christian college or seminary when he was younger, then reading through the Old Testament would have been a rewarding spiritual exercise. Anyone involved with Christian education, however, knows that is probably a wrong assumption. Survey courses on the Old Testament taught in Christian schools often require students to memorize the books of the Bible, the names and dates of the patriarchs, the judges, the kings and prophets of both the northern and southern kingdoms, the arguments of critics and the rebuttals to them. Although these subjects have their place in a curriculum, basic courses should create in students a love for the Old Testament and an awareness of what impact it can make on their lives. Unfortunately, they often fail to do so. Who really cares much, students wonder, about the exploits and musings of old dead kings or the diatribes of some angry prophets?

To complicate matters, professors sometimes teach over their students' heads and hearts. They overestimate the knowledge modern young people—even those from religious homes—possess about the Scriptures. In one Old Testament introduction class, for instance, a teacher delivered a well-developed lecture on the evidence for an early date for the book of Daniel only to have a student ask after class, "Was Daniel a character in the Bible?" It's hard to imagine such students ever coming to exclaim with David, "Oh, how I love your law! I meditate on it all day long." Aside from a familiar verse or two, they do not think much about the Old Testament at all.

John Walton and Andrew Hill in *Old Testament Today* observe that many students find their experience with the Old Testament something like playing the piñata game. "There is a target out there they are aiming at, but they are blindfolded and turned around so many times they are disoriented. They flail wildly at the air and become frustrated with an exercise that offers so little in return for their efforts."[1]

Bewilderment about the Old Testament doesn't only infect laypeople or college and seminary students. Many men and women who have taken graduate studies in Old Testament or Semitics have gotten through the courses but in the process emerged with a diploma and a badly damaged trust in the Scriptures. In many graduate schools the text of the Old Testament is simply not taken at its face value. Instead the text is treated as a scissors and paste job put together by some unknown ancient editors. The characteristic assumption in those studies is that the biblical books are at best distorted historical records, and behind the manuscripts of the Old Testament there are lost manuscripts that preceded what we have now. Existing texts, therefore, are merely residue of what has been lost under ancient dust. Higher criticism with its assumptions has lowered rather than elevated the respect educated people have for the Scriptures. It has made laughable any assertion that the different books of the Old Testament have overarching themes that bind them together.

The study of the Old Testament has also been hindered as much by its friends as by its critics. Ministers who would defend to the death the inspiration and authority of the Scriptures ignore huge sections of the First Testament in their preaching. While they may occasionally preach from a few familiar psalms or draw lessons, sometimes dubious, from the stories in Genesis or from the lives of Samuel, David, or Nehemiah, they avoid other sections of the Old Testament such as Deuteronomy, Leviticus, Proverbs, Ecclesiastes, and most of the Major and Minor Prophets. These are the white pages of the Bible, filled with names we can't pronounce, living in places we have never heard of, so we don't bother to read them.

We also ignore these sections because we don't know how to handle them. Preachers, like other people, have stereotypes of God and how he should act. When we come to passages where God does not conform to our code of behavior or to episodes where he says things that we feel are not proper for God to say, we are convinced that the problem is in the Bible and not with us. We form a "Canon within the Canon" and deal only with those passages that don't raise a ruckus or make listeners feel uncomfortable.

Barbara Brown Taylor reported on what happened when she was invited to speak to a senior citizens' group on "Women in the Old Testament." She told them about Jael, who drove a tent peg through Sisera's temple, and Esther, who won permission for the Jews to destroy seventy-five thousand of their enemies. "They thanked me very much," Taylor said, "and never asked me back."[2]

One well-known evangelical minister explained why he seldom takes a text directly from the Old Testament. He preaches from the New Testament, he says, and uses the Old Testament as a source for illustrations. In that way he feels he exposes his congregation to "the whole counsel of God." That approach seems deficient in at least two ways. First, homiletically it ignores the basic principle of illustration: we illustrate the unknown with the known. If an illustration has to be explained, don't use it. Because most passages of the Old Testament have to be explained in detail to a modern audience, using Old Testament stories as illustrations takes unfamiliar incidents in the Old Testament to explain or apply an unclear text in the New. More important, however, reducing the Old Testament to an anthology of illustrations for sermons based on the Gospels or the Epistles slights the Old Testament authors who were theologians in their own right. They were skilled authors who conveyed God's message through such genres as story, proverb, and poetry, and their messages had their own purposes, but certainly they did not write to provide illustrations for other biblical writers.

Congregations who have seldom listened to preaching that opened up the Old Testament or who have only heard sermons drawing practical lessons based on the lives of ancient heroes may be excused for dismissing two-thirds of the Canon as unimportant and irrelevant. Though a pastor may not have said it to them directly, people in the pew come to feel that the good stuff is in the New Testament. It would never occur to them that the Old Testament was the only Bible Jesus knew and it was the Scripture of the early church.

Avoiding the Old Testament resembles strolling into the theater for the final act of a play and ignoring completely what the play is really about. It is to assume the playwright wouldn't expect anyone to take the first two acts of the play seriously.

In spite of the fact that the Old Testament has suffered at the hands of its critics and its friends, we must not ignore it. We must know and preach it. "The Old Testament has been handed down to us in the church as a priceless treasure," says Elizabeth Achtemeier. In it our Israelite forebears in the faith have preserved for us some eighteen hundred years of their witness to what the one God has said and done in their lives. Through their faithful testimony, the Holy One of Israel, who is at the same time the God and Father of our Lord Jesus Christ, has revealed himself. Through the words of his historians and prophets, psalmists and wisdom teachers, priests and lawgivers, God has formed our faith, instructed our piety in proper reverence and awe, awakened our expectations of his working, and bent our wills to his desires and goals. Apart from the Old Testament, we do not know who the Father of Jesus Christ is, nor do we know who we are as "the Israel of God" (Gal. 6:16).[3]

No one has been more insistent than Walter Kaiser that the church today desperately needs the Old Testament. He has spent his adult life learning the languages of Scripture and the message of those sacred Writings, and then he has taught what he knows to those who teach on seminary faculties, pastors, and men and women in the pews. He has carried out his mission by serving on the faculties of Wheaton College, Trinity Evangelical Divinity School, and Gordon-Conwell Theological Seminary. In those positions he has left a thumbprint on thousands of graduates who in turn serve on faculties and in churches around the world. He has written over thirty books directed to scholars and thoughtful laypeople that tackle the hard questions asked by people who want to take the Old Testament seriously. He has preached from the Old Testament in countless churches and Bible conferences and weekly in chapel at Gordon-Conwell Theological Seminary. Audiences respond not only to the content of his sermons but to his humor and down-to-life way of speaking.

It is fitting that this volume honoring Walter Kaiser should be written by a group of authors who have either sat in his classes or taught by his side. It is fitting, too, that they should write about "Preaching the Old Testament." If the truth of the Old Testament is to sound again in churches, it must be from their pulpits. Perhaps this collection of essays will ignite a spark that causes to blaze again the warm, strong, relevant preaching of the entire Word of God. If under God that should happen, nothing would please Walter Kaiser more.

Introduction

Kaiser Is the Key Word

Scott M. Gibson

This book is intended to give seminary students and pastors the tools they need to preach from the Old Testament. The focus of each chapter is on what it takes to prepare to preach a sermon. The emphasis is on preparation. The question that guided the selection of material and aided the authors in their writing is this: What do seminarians and pastors need to know as they begin to prepare to preach from Old Testament genres? The authors in this book are all preachers and scholars who themselves have thought about the necessary tools and information students and pastors require to preach appropriately from the First Testament.

The grouping of authors is intentional. All of the authors have the Old Testament in common. But more than this, they have a person in common: Walter C. Kaiser Jr. The book is intended to be a resource for preachers, but it is also an occasion to honor one of the most noted contemporary Old Testament scholars of our day, Dr. Walter C. Kaiser Jr. He is, in one word, the reason for this project. Kaiser is the key word.

What do I mean by *key word*? Most students and colleagues of Walter Kaiser are aware of his commitment to the "key word" approach in preaching. This respected style of preaching was developed by Charles W. Koller of Northern Baptist Theological Seminary in Chicago during the middle twentieth century. Koller had two colleagues who were also his disciples in the field of homiletics, Farris Whitesell and Lloyd Perry. The three professors, Koller, Whitesell, and Perry, led a thriving doctor of theology in preaching program at Northern Baptist. Both Whitesell and Perry published widely, but Perry was the one who championed the key word method in extensive publishing of articles and books, in addition to the broad influence he had on his students.

A graduate of Drs. Koller, Whitesell, and Perry's doctor of theology in preaching program was Neil Ayers Winegarden. Dr. Winegarden taught preaching to the young Walter Kaiser while he was studying for his Master of Divinity degree at Wheaton College Graduate School. The key word approach became Kaiser's. From that time on Walter Kaiser embraced and developed the template championed by his teacher at Wheaton, and those from whom he learned it.

Interestingly, Lloyd Perry eventually left Northern Baptist Theological Seminary to teach for a short while at Gordon Divinity School in Wenham, Massachusetts. From there Perry went back to the Midwest to continue his teaching career at Trinity Evangelical Divinity School in Deerfield, Illinois, where he became a colleague of Walter Kaiser.

Dr. Kaiser found key word preaching to be an exegetical and homiletical organizing principle. As for the emphasis of the text and how the key word functions in putting one's exegesis into clear organization for preaching, Kaiser asserts, "Whenever a series of sentences or clauses is linked together by the same introductory word ('because,' 'since,' 'therefore,' or the like), it may be possible to organize the message around these key words." He states further, "In this case each major point in the sermon will be a development of the subject from the same perspective and angle."[1]

Not only is Walter Kaiser an Old Testament scholar, but also he is a preacher, a world-renowned communicator. He has shared his joy of God's Word with thousands of students, churches, and conference attendees. His numerous books underscore his double investment in the study of God's Word and the communication of it. When one thinks of Old Testament studies, one thinks of Walter Kaiser. When one thinks of Old Testament preaching, one thinks of Walter Kaiser. Why? Because Kaiser, Walter C. Kaiser, is the key word.

Challenges to Preaching the Old Testament

Scott M. Gibson

Barriers to Preaching from the Old Testament

This book is about equipping preachers who must prepare to preach from the books of the Old Testament. However, when preachers are faced with whether they will preach from the Old Testament or the New Testament, some will choose the New Testament, rather than the First Testament. Preachers would rather preach from the crusty Paul than from the distant Moses. Why is it that some Christian preachers favor preaching from the New Testament? A casual discussion among preachers revealed the following reasons why some preachers avoid preaching from the Old Testament: Hebrew is harder than Greek; the Old Testament culture is foreign; the Old Testament is irrelevant; we just like the New Testament better than the Old Testament; we do not need the Old Testament because we have Christ. Listen in on the composite conversations I had with several preachers.

Hebrew Is Harder than Greek

"Hebrew is harder than Greek!" stated one pastor, while another said, "We know Greek better than Hebrew." Still another pastor confessed, "It takes too much work and study and we don't make the time." One reason why preachers do not preach from the Old Testament, according to one pastor, is that "it contains genres we don't know how to preach."

But the reality is this, according to another pastor: "There is a lack of understanding about how much the New Testament writers actually depended upon, and were influenced by, the Old Testament." Pastors genuinely struggle with preaching from the older Testament. Certainly, the issue of language facility is a challenge. In light of this, one pastor commented, "Preachers avoid preaching from the Old Testament because it seems more intimidating than the New Testament." Hebrew appears harder than Greek. The work of translation and exegesis at times appears too daunting to the preacher.

"I still know that an upcoming series in the Old Testament will take more preparation time for me than a New Testament series," concluded a Midwest pastor. A pastor in the South agreed: "It's easier to prepare a sermon from the New Testament. The units of thought aren't as long. Sometimes in the Old Testament the immediate context can be several chapters." For these pastors, Hebrew is harder than Greek.

Old Testament Culture Is Foreign

"We can't relate to the culture," said one preacher. We fear the Old Testament because we do not know it. Preachers may feel that they will never really understand the complexities of Old Testament ritual and theology. The complicated laws, the beautiful poetry, and the difficult prophecies heighten a preacher's fears of clearly communicating what this part of the Bible is all about.

The difficulty is this: preachers and people have a tough time relating to the culture of the Old Testament. "We can't pronounce the names," remarked one pastor half jokingly. But upon further reflection, he mused, "Perhaps there's more truth to this than we will admit."

Another pastor commented, "The Old Testament is more removed from our times socially, culturally, and covenantally, and therefore harder for us to understand and access." He had a person in his church ask about the test for the unfaithful wife in Numbers 5. In that chapter a wife suspected of adultery is made to drink dirty water and then is observed to see if gastrointestinal pain results. "Isn't that test a little stacked against her?" the church member asked the pastor. The pastor concluded, "Questions like this one reveal theological and gender difficulties that are hard for the preacher to tackle."

A pastor from the West agreed: "It is harder for people to relate to Hebrew culture than Greek culture. There are issues like war and polygamy to deal with." Another pastor from the West chimed in, "The Old Testament is rooted in cultures very foreign to that of its contemporary audiences." He continued, "It addresses issues like the Babylonian captivity that contemporary listeners will never face." But one African-American pastor observed that "African-American culture is a story-telling culture, like the Old Testament. And stories of redemption run throughout its pages."

A Midwest pastor remarked, "The theological complexities in the Old Testament are often too difficult, and we don't want to touch them in the pulpit." "Who can understand the prophets anyway?" questioned another pastor. And since the prophets are difficult, preaching from the Old Testament may become too challenging for preachers to tackle. In addition, the issue of time for preparation can be a struggle. One pastor from the South stated, "Speaking for myself, I'm more familiar with the broader contexts of most of the New Testament books and don't have to spend as much time in preparation. To preach from most Old Testament books requires additional reading and study of the backgrounds of the books." For some pastors, Old Testament culture is foreign for them—and for their listeners.

The Old Testament Is Irrelevant

"The Old Testament is just that, old," a preacher might say. "I want to be relevant to my listeners. They struggle to see the importance of the New Testament, let alone the Old." A pastor from New England pinpointed the underlying prejudice: "It's out of date." Still another pastor observed, "Given our preoccupation with the pragmatic, 'how to,' 'purpose driven' approach to preaching, much of the Old Testament doesn't seem to fit the contemporary 'niche' market." "Preachers do not see in the Old Testament any relevance to the needs of today's congregations," remarked one pastor.

A preacher from the Mid-Atlantic confessed, "For me the struggle is always the potential for problems in application. I always feel like I am making huge jumps in application. The New Testament is much easier to apply."

"Many of the Old Testament laws do not apply to us, or we find it confusing to determine how they apply," voiced one pastor. Said a pastor from the South, "It's more dangerous to preach from the Old Testament. (It is easier to abuse it.) It seems easier to moralize or exemplarize from Old Testament passages, and it's easy to confuse what applies only to Israel and what applies to both Israel and us today."

The ease of New Testament applicability over the Old Testament seems to be a common perception among pastors. "It's relatively easy to see the everyday application of Jesus's sermon on the mount or the epistles," remarked one pastor. "But the prophets, that's not as transparent." Relevance of the Old Testament is an issue for some pastors.

Favoring the New Testament over the Old Testament

A preacher from the South said, "Preachers often know the New Testament better—and we are quick to preach that which we know best since it makes for easier preparation; perhaps the preacher's congregation knows the New Testament better." "Besides," stated one pastor, "there's a problem in the Old Testament with provincial language that favors Israel, but where does it leave us?"

For most evangelicals the simple reason the New Testament is favored over the Old Testament is, in the words of a New England pastor, "The New Testament seems more familiar—not as long ago and far away as the Old Testament." Agreeing, a pastor from the South observed, "Sometimes, it seems easier to bring about application from New Testament passages." But he continued, "That may not be true in reality, but it seems so." Still another pastor commented plainly, "Pastors may not have an interest in the Old Testament."

A solution to this problem is suggested by one pastor: "I think that preachers tend not to read the Scriptures as broadly, deeply, and devotionally as would be ideal. I believe that if preachers immersed themselves in the teaching of the entire Scriptures, not just to be able to preach it well, but primarily to hear from God and to allow one's soul to be fed, people would preach more from the Old Testament." But as preachers, we may favor the New Testament over the Old Testament.

No Need for the Old Testament Because We Have Christ

"Where is the message of Christ in the Old Testament?" a preacher may ask. He or she wants to preach Christ, not Old Testament poems and prophecies. Preachers may avoid preaching from the Old Testament because Christ completed that which the Old Testament required. One pastor noted, "I find it harder to make direct connections to Christ, especially if I need to give an invitation at the end of every sermon." A reason why preachers avoid preaching from the Old Testament is, as one preacher stated, "There's a perceived lack of need to preach the Old Testament since we live in a post-Christ age."

One pastor remembered, "In my first church, a man spread a rumor that I didn't really believe in Jesus. When I eventually confronted him about it, he said, 'Since you've been here, you've spent half your time preaching from the Old Testament.'" The pastor concluded, "He ended up leaving for a 'New Testament church.'"

Pastors and people tend to be more comfortable with Jesus and Paul than with Moses and David. "I think most Christians are more familiar with the New Testament and so the exegesis is easier," said a pastor from the West. He continued, "Also the New Testament obviously talks more about Christ, whereas, depending on your interpretation of the Old Testament, it is harder to overtly find Christ there." A pastor from New England agreed, "I wonder if preachers don't know what to do with Jesus when it comes to the Old Testament. How does he fit in to the Old Testament?"

Some preachers and people in their congregations think biblical history began with the New Testament. Oddly, they do not see the connection with Old Testament history as Matthew begins his Gospel with the genealogy of Christ. What to do with Christ is always a challenge for preachers when they preach from the Old Testament.

Helping Preachers Preach from the Old Testament

The purpose of this book is to help preachers cultivate a desire and skill to preach from the Old Testament. The various chapters are developed to help the struggling preacher prepare sermons from the various genres of Old Testament literature and to expand his or her understanding of the Old Testament in light of its history, culture, relationship with the New Testament, and potential for preaching.

The above barriers to preaching the Old Testament are addressed in this book by first helping pastors refresh their Hebrew skills and encouraging them to keep them healthy. Dennis Magary carefully guides pastors back to the original language, urging them to use their possibly rusty Hebrew to construct fresh and vibrantly informed sermons. Yes, it does take work. And those who have taken the time to learn Hebrew will once again see the importance of wrestling with the language for sermon preparation.

From the development of healthy Hebrew, readers then move into a study of what preachers need to know in order to preach from various books and genres in the Old Testament. The chapters include studies in preparing to preach from the historical books (Carol Kaminski), narratives (Jeffrey Arthurs), the Old Testament Law (Douglas Stuart), Psalms and Proverbs (Duane Garrett), and the Prophets (John Sailhamer).

The objection by some preachers—that Old Testament culture is foreign—is dealt with skillfully in the chapter on "Preaching the Old Testament in Light of Its Culture" by Timothy Laniak. And even though preachers tend to favor the New Testament, Roy Ciampa helps preachers to see the connection between the Testaments in his study, "Toward the Effective Preaching of New Testament Texts That Cite the Old Testament." In addition, both David Larsen and Robert Coleman demonstrate the relevance of preaching the Old Testament. Larsen concentrates on "Preaching the Old Testament Today," while Coleman focuses on "Preaching the Old Testament Evangelistically."

Preparing to Preach

A Midwest pastor observed, "The unfamiliar names, customs, and events keep preachers from doing more with the Old Testament. We realize that more background information is needed for us in study preparation and for our listeners, and that takes time away from exposition and application." The following chapters are intended to help preachers, like this one, tackle the various challenges of preaching the Old Testament. The hope is that readers will not be intimidated by the richness of the First Testament but will be able to preach it with confidence and care. The emphasis in planning and preaching is balance. Yet, some readers may end up like two pastors from the West. One stated, "I preach most of the time from the Old Testament, because so much emphasis has been put on the New Testament." The other declared, "I am estimating that during the next year, 70 percent of my preaching at my church will come from Old Testament texts."

My desire as editor of this volume is that preachers who have avoided preaching from the Old Testament will be encouraged to do it again because they now know what it means to prepare to preach it.

2

Keeping Your Hebrew Healthy

Dennis R. Magary

What if you had the opportunity to read for yourself the most important words ever written? What if you could learn the language of those words so that you could read them as they were first written? What if you could then spend your life reading those words, studying those words, understanding those words, telling others about those words—the most important words ever written? Every time a student enrolls for a course in biblical Hebrew, the potentiality of the "what if" becomes a reality.

Learning biblical Hebrew is a challenge. But learning the language is not the greatest challenge. Academic incentive is a great motivator. As long as there are quizzes to take and exercises to write, as long as there is a grade riding on what you do, and there is a professor to whom you must give account, staying with the language and succeeding somehow stays within reach. But what happens when there are no longer quizzes or exercises or professors or grades? In his foreword to David Baker's *More*

Light on the Path, Eugene Peterson captures the all-too-common fate of the biblical languages in the real world:

> Post-academic life is demanding and decidedly unsympathetic to anything that doesn't provide quick and obvious returns. We are handed job descriptions in which our wonderful languages don't even rate a footnote; we acquire families who plunge us into urgencies in which Hebrew radicals provide no shortcuts; we can't keep up with all the stuff thrown at us in easy English—who has time for hard Greek? It isn't long before the languages are, as we say, "lost."[1]

The most important thing pastors and teachers do in any given week is communicate to people what God has said. The most sacred moments they spend in ministry are the moments in which they are proclaiming the Word of God—the most important words ever written! The man or woman who has the responsibility to communicate to others what God has said needs to *know* exactly what God has said! A challenge far greater than learning Hebrew is keeping it vital and healthy for use in lifelong ministry. The whole point of studying Hebrew and Greek in seminary is to be able to have direct access to the biblical text—the very foundation for Christian faith and practice—in the languages in which God's Word was originally given.

As fine as our contemporary translations are, as carefully as they have been prepared, a translation is still a translation. It is and will always be at least one step removed from the original. An English version, a translation of the Hebrew text in any language, is an interpretation, a commentary reflecting critical and interpretive decisions by a host of scholars. Translators have made numerous decisions regarding the meaning of words, the syntax of clauses, the referent of a pronoun. Where the text is ambiguous, the translator decides whether or not to clarify. Where a Hebrew text introduces a tension, the translator faces the decision of whether or not to resolve the tension.

Because translators aim to make the text understandable to the reader, the decisions they make ultimately affect interpretation. This is not to cast aspersions on translators, for were it not for their diligence and devotion to making the Word of God available in the languages of "all the families of the earth," how could any of us know what God has said to us? But those whom God has raised up to speak his Word, to explain to each age what he has revealed to us about himself and what we need to know to live life before him, these men and women need to understand what he has said. The ability to read and study the Scriptures in the languages in which they were written ensures a more accurate understanding.

This chapter will address the challenge faced by everyone who at one point in life studied biblical Hebrew, determined that upon graduation they would use it in ministry, only to find that their Hebrew has been "lost." We will explore how you can revitalize the Hebrew you learned and maintain a working knowledge of biblical Hebrew for lifelong ministry. In the sections that follow, I will propose strategies for concrete ways you can appropriate and retain Hebrew language skill and develop greater proficiency in the use of the biblical Hebrew.

Strategy for Reclaiming Biblical Hebrew— Where to Begin

An important place to begin is to give thoughtful consideration to how you learn best. Classroom approaches to teaching biblical Hebrew have traditionally given little thought to this crucial factor. Hebrew teachers have a tendency to teach in the way they were taught. Learning biblical Hebrew requires mastery of vocabulary and grammar. Hebrew vocabulary needs to be memorized. Noun and verb forms need to be recognized. So the assignment is made and the instructions are given: "Learn the vocabulary in Lesson 16, and be prepared for a quiz on any form of the hollow verb." If a student should ask, "Can you make some suggestions as to how we might 'prepare'?" the answer has all too often come back, "Just memorize them!" This approach is conducive neither to mastery of the essentials nor to lifelong use of the language.

The past three decades have yielded a significant body of literature on learning styles.[2] Although the impetus for the research has been interest in the needs of children who are learning challenged, the context for the research has been the broader educational community, and the results have been insightful. This, of course, is not the venue to discuss learning modalities, but a few observations will be helpful for our purposes.

The identification of distinct learning styles has precipitated awareness among educators that individuals learn differently and that people learn most effectively when they can learn according to their learning style. Although the research has shown that there is a spectrum of learning styles, three basic learning modalities have been identified. Some people are predominantly auditory learners. They learn best what they *hear*. This individual will memorize by repeating information aloud over and over. This person will need to hear himself say something in order to remember it. This kind of learner benefits tremendously by listening to recordings.

Other people are visual learners. They learn best what they *see*. Such people will need to see an image or an illustration of what they are being taught before adequately understanding it. This individual will try to get a mental picture of what is being read or said. This kind of learner benefits from illustrations and tables that distill and summarize information.

Still other people are kinesthetic learners. They learn best what they *do*. Learning for these people is facilitated by motion. Because this person has difficulty sitting still, the kinesthetic learner learns best by physically participating in a task.

The study of Hebrew vocabulary will provide a good example of these distinctive learning styles. Each type of learner will approach maintaining a good working vocabulary differently. Auditory learners will need to repeat vocabulary words aloud in order to commit them to memory. They can best remember vocabulary words they hear. The auditory learner will benefit from an audio resource like vocabulary words recorded on CD.

Visual learners need to see, rather than hear, vocabulary words. The visual learner will find vocabulary cards to be a more useful resource than an audio CD. This person may need actually to write the Hebrew word several times to commit it to memory. The visual learner, who tends to be drawn to colorful, stimulating objects, may even color-code his cards, for instance, verbs highlighted in green (for movement, action!), nouns highlighted in yellow, adjectives in orange.

Kinesthetic learners may find they can learn and review vocabulary most effectively when they are on the move. Working through a set of vocabulary cards while out walking will be far more productive for them than reviewing them while sitting at a desk. Kinesthetic learners will remember more words by listening to vocabulary on CD while biking or jogging than they will by studying quietly in the library. The kinesthetic learner might even use hand gestures or another form of body language to enhance memory.

Each learning style has its own characteristics. Although one learning style will tend to be dominant in an individual, the human brain is complex, so a person will benefit most by appropriating techniques from less dominant learning styles as well. One learning modality does not preclude the others. Maximal learning will occur when there is a blend of approaches. So, to reclaim the Hebrew you once had, to revitalize the Hebrew you worked so hard to learn, begin by asking yourself, "How do I learn best?" You will augment your efforts to keep your Hebrew healthy by giving thoughtful consideration to how you learn most effectively, and then, by adopting techniques and utilizing tools and resources that correspond with your learning style.

We now turn our attention to specific strategies for keeping your Hebrew healthy. We will propose strategies on two fronts. Strategies for *review* will address the importance of revisiting the fundamentals of the language, especially vocabulary and grammar. Strategies for *use*, or text-focused strategies, will speak to the importance of regular Hebrew use and engagement with the biblical Hebrew texts. Strategies will include a combination of technology and traditional resources.

Keeping Your Hebrew Healthy by Reviewing It—Element-Focused Strategies

Vocabulary Building

Vocabulary always poses a formidable challenge to learning any language and retaining it. Miles V. Van Pelt and Gary D. Pratico indicate that there are a total of 8,679 "lexical items" in the vocabulary of biblical Hebrew.[3] The total number of "distinct words" offered by Andersen and Forbes is somewhat higher at 9,980.[4] However, more than 7,500 of those words occur fewer than ten times. This means that a working vocabulary of roughly one-fourth of the total vocabulary of the Hebrew Bible equips one to translate the Hebrew text without constantly looking up words. The statistics offered by Van Pelt and Pratico put these numbers in perspective:

> By memorizing only the first fifty words in the frequency vocabulary list, students will be equipped to recognize almost 55% of the total words that occur in the Hebrew Old Testament (419,687). Students who master the 641 words that occur fifty or more times will be able to recognize over 80% of all words. Finally, those who are brave enough to master all 1,903 words in the frequency vocabulary list will be equipped to recognize almost 90% of all words that occur in the Hebrew Old Testament. In other words, memorization of only 22% of the total stock of Hebrew vocabulary (1,903 out of 8,679 total lexical items) will enable a student to recognize 90% of all words appearing in the Hebrew Bible. The remaining 6,776 lexical items occur only 49,914 total times, a figure significantly less than the number of occurrences of the Hebrew conjunction *wᵉ* (and).[5]

Indeed, even a modest working vocabulary provides a solid foundation for reading and regular use of the Hebrew text of the Old Testament.

How does one acquire and retain even a modest working vocabulary? The keys are (1) review and (2) usage. Vocabulary words must be committed to memory. Ultimately, though, regular review and usage is how the words and their meanings are retained. Several tools are available to help one succeed in the building and mastery of vocabulary. Larry A. Mitchel's *A Student's Vocabulary for Biblical Hebrew and Aramaic* provides frequency lists for all words occurring ten or more times in the Hebrew Bible (with the exception of proper nouns that occur fewer than fifty times).[6] All words include definitions and a pronunciation guide. George M. Landes's *Building Your Biblical Hebrew Vocabulary: Learning Words by Frequency and Cognate* provides more nuanced frequency lists.[7] The lists in Landes are arranged on the basis of the frequency of the verbal root. Nominal and other cognates are then listed under each root:

> It has been my experience that the task [of learning biblical Hebrew vocabulary] is somewhat easier when one can see the words in groupings that show their etymological relationships, thus providing a helpful mnemonic device for learning how cognate words are meaningfully linked.[8]

There is certainly an advantage to focusing on words that are etymologically related. But even Landes recognizes the possible disadvantage: "Of course, this means that one will most often be learning cognate words that may have quite radically different frequencies so that the student may not master all the higher frequency words first."[9] Also available is Van Pelt and Pratico's *The Vocabulary Guide to Biblical Hebrew*.[10] Van Pelt and Pratico offer the most venues for vocabulary study. The primary list of *The Vocabulary Guide* is comprised of Hebrew words arranged by frequency and includes all Hebrew words that occur ten or more times in the Old Testament (excluding proper nouns). Subsequent lists include various alphabetical listings, like words arranged by common root (cognate), proper nouns, segholate pattern nouns, adjectives, prepositions, verbs, and subsets of the verb.

Additional vocabulary resources for both auditory and visual learners are also available for review and reference. Boxed sets of vocabulary cards make it easy to review vocabulary anywhere. *Old Testament Hebrew Vocabulary Cards* prepared by Miles V. Van Pelt[11] contains all words that occur thirty or more times in the Hebrew Bible. The one thousand cards are keyed to the elementary Hebrew grammars of Van Pelt and Pratico, Mark

Futato,[12] Allen Ross,[13] and C. L. Seow.[14] The *Biblical Hebrew Vocabulary Cards* prepared by Raymond B. Dillard cover over 1,200 words from the vocabulary of the Hebrew Bible. This set includes 978 cards, which cover all nouns, adjectives, and verbs occurring twenty-five or more times, along with prepositions, adverbs, and particles. Vocabulary cards are convenient to use, and cards within a set can be organized and manipulated according to the needs of the reviewer.

Also available for vocabulary review is an audio resource by Jonathan T. Pennington. *Old Testament Hebrew Vocabulary*, a set of two audio CDs, contains a reading of all Hebrew words that occur twenty or more times in the Old Testament, each with proper pronunciation and an English definition.[15]

Hebrew vocabulary in electronic format is rapidly becoming the delivery system of choice. *BibleWorks Version 6*[16] includes a Hebrew vocabulary flashcard module that makes it possible to sort words for study and review on the basis of frequency of occurrence, part of speech, portion of Scripture, or learned status (either "learned" or "not learned"). Other features of this utility, like the ability to add a sound file to each word in the default word lists, make the *BibleWorks* vocabulary flashcard feature an effective tool for learning and maintaining a strong Hebrew vocabulary. Beyond this, Van Pelt and Pratico are promising an electronic version of their vocabulary guide. "Students will be able to hear, sort, practice, and review their vocabulary on the computer in an interactive environment."[17]

As we have stated, Hebrew vocabulary will be learned and retained most effectively when the mode of study and review is in keeping with one's personal learning style. Resources for vocabulary study abound and are now available for all modalities of learning.

Suggested Strategy: Determine your target frequency—words occurring fifty or more times is good, thirty or more times is better, ten or more times is best. Review your Hebrew vocabulary regularly. Start with the highest frequency words and move methodically toward the lower frequencies. Resources such as Mitchel or Van Pelt and Pratico will be most useful here. Focus on five words each day (Monday through Friday). If you use vocabulary cards, carry the selected five words with you and refer to them throughout the day. At the end of each week (Saturday) review the twenty-five words you have studied. Pull out any words you have not yet mastered and distribute those among the new daily words for the next week. At the end of four weeks, review the words that you have studied over those weeks (approximately one hundred). Continue this study/review cycle until you reach your target frequency. If you started with a target frequency of words occurring fifty or more times, and you achieve that goal, set a new target. Work your way down gradually to words occurring ten or more times. At the point you are able to recognize almost 90 percent of all words that occur in the biblical Hebrew text, you will have achieved a substantial reading vocabulary; and that is what you will be able to do when you open your Hebrew Bible—read!

Morphology and Syntax

A good working vocabulary is essential to the well-being of your Hebrew, but maintaining a robust vocabulary is not sufficient. Regular review of morphology and syntax is also necessary, particularly in the early stages of Hebrew "rehabilitation." With the passage of time, particularly time spent away from the language, it is easy to forget elements of Hebrew grammar. The basic structure and formation of Hebrew words once known well is now less familiar. The way Hebrew words combine into phrases and clauses and the ways that these combine to form sentences can too easily be lost. A sustained review of the rudiments of Hebrew grammar can revitalize and even reenergize one's understanding of biblical Hebrew. More resources are available now than ever before to facilitate productive review and augment one's understanding of the language.

Review of the Basics—Start at the Beginning

A good place to begin—it would seem—would be to revisit an old friend, your elementary Hebrew textbook. The assumption here, of course, is that your textbook was a "good friend." That may or may not be the case. A fresh start offers all the advantages of a new endeavor, minus the disadvantages. Looking at familiar material in a new way or from a different perspective can actually facilitate review. The joy of discovery, or rediscovery, can precipitate very positive results without the unnecessary reminder of past academic struggles or learning unpleasantries triggered by your old textbook.

A better starting point, one that engages both auditory and visual modes of learning, is *Hebrew Tutor for Multimedia CD-ROM*.[18] This interactive software program offers instruction in the elements of Hebrew grammar, the equivalent of first-year Hebrew. *Hebrew Tutor* has proven its effectiveness as a teaching tool. It is particularly well suited for anyone who wishes to review the fundamentals of the language. Each of the fourteen chapters offers four learning levels: (1) *learn*, with outlines covering aspects of grammar and morphology, (2) *drill*, with practice, (3) *exercise*, with spelling and reading, and (4) *review*, with charts.

Hebrew Tutor provides two learning methods. The sequential learning method moves through the four learning levels, one lesson at a time. The overview learning method, ideal for review, takes the user through the *learn* level of all fourteen chapters, then the through the *drill* level of all fourteen chapters, and so on through the *exercise* and *review* levels. In addition, *Hebrew Tutor* includes the entire text of the book of Ruth, complete with identification of all forms and pronunciation and readings of the text.

Another resource to supplement your review is Donald R. Vance's *A Hebrew Reader for Ruth*.[19] It offers the user identifications, annotations of forms, as well as references to selected standard grammars, and it can be used effectively in conjunction with *Hebrew Tutor*.

A helpful resource for review of basic Hebrew grammar is available in Gary A. Long's *Grammatical Concepts 101 for Biblical Hebrew: Learning Biblical Hebrew Grammatical Concepts Through English Grammar*.[20] Long's approach complements the standard teaching grammars by taking the student back to concepts of English grammar as a way of learning basic concepts that are specific to Hebrew grammar. Each chapter begins with clear definitions, descriptions, and illustrations of a grammatical concept in English and then describes and illustrates the same concept in Hebrew. The strategy of illustrating English alongside a language to be learned is not new, but Long's appropriation of this method for learning biblical Hebrew is unique and effective.

At the intermediate level, Ben Zvi, Hancock, and Beinert's *Readings in Biblical Hebrew: An Intermediate Textbook* provides a helpful review of Hebrew morphology and syntax by inductive analysis of biblical texts.[21] Although Ben Zvi's work follows the pedagogical approach and utilizes the terminology of Bonnie Kittel's introductory grammar, *Biblical Hebrew: A Text and Workbook*,[22] students who learned biblical Hebrew with a different textbook will find no difficulty using *Readings in Biblical Hebrew*. Ben Zvi's volume is generously cross-referenced to the elementary grammars of Moshe Greenberg,[23] Page H. Kelley,[24] Thomas O. Lambdin,[25] C. L. Seow,[26] and Jacob Weingreen.[27] For more detailed discussion of grammatical points, the user is directed to the intermediate and advanced grammars of Gesenius-Kautzsch-Cowley,[28] Joüon-Muraoka,[29] and Waltke and O'Connor.[30] *Readings in Biblical Hebrew* offers readings in the historical books, legal material, prophetic literature, wisdom writings, and the Psalms. The length of the passages varies, as does their difficulty.

Suggested Strategy: Start with a comprehensive review of morphology—basic forms and endings, pronominal prefixes and suffixes. Move next to basic forms in context. *Hebrew Tutor* provides an excellent format for initial review. Whether you use the sequential or overview method of learning, the combination of both visual and auditory presentation maximizes contact with the language. The sequential method is probably best to start with, allowing focused review and practice on one aspect of morphology before tackling another. This initial review will be foundational to what you are able to do later.

Gain confidence with the outlines and exercises before moving on. When you transition to forms in context, use the Ruth text in *Hebrew Tutor*. Pace yourself at one verse per day, approximately ten minutes for this phase of review. Working your way through the four chapters of Ruth will provide a good review of basic grammar and vocabulary in context. Use the following approach as a guide: (1) Listen. Click on **Play** and listen to the reading of an entire verse in Hebrew. (2) Pronunciation, Identification, Translation. Click on each Hebrew word of the verse and listen to the pronunciation. Note its parsing or identification and translation. (3) Listen. Click on **Play** and listen again to the reading of the entire verse in Hebrew. (4) Repeat. Click on each Hebrew word of the verse, listen to the pronunciation, and this time, repeat the word after the *Hebrew Tutor* reader. (5) Listen. Click on **Play** and listen again to the reading of the entire verse in Hebrew. (6) Read. Now, read the verse aloud in its entirety in Hebrew. (7) Listen. Finally, click on **Play** and listen one final time to the reading of the entire verse in Hebrew. Consult Vance for additional annotation of forms. Working methodically, one verse at a time, one verse per day, through the text of Ruth will revitalize your understanding of the rudiments of Hebrew grammar. Follow up your work in *Hebrew Tutor* with the more aggressive, advanced inductive review available in Ben Zvi, Hancock, and Beinert's *Readings in Biblical Hebrew*.

Completing this proposed course of sustained review of both vocabulary and basic morphology and syntax will take about eight months and will position you for significant advances in reading comprehension and engagement with the biblical Hebrew text.

Reacquaint Yourself with the Reference Literature of Hebrew Grammar and Syntax

Suggesting that one "read" a Hebrew grammar may seem pedantic. Intermediate and advanced grammars in biblical Hebrew are designed primarily for reference. Of course, reading an intermediate or advanced grammar is not the way to "learn" biblical Hebrew. But for anyone who has had a year of elementary Hebrew and a course or two in Hebrew exegesis, a sustained reading of a Hebrew grammar can bring a level of linguistic understanding not possible in the early days when you were still struggling to remember a myriad of forms for the next quiz. The grammar will clarify the function of forms and structures within the language, the understanding of which is key to using Hebrew as a vital part of one's ministry.

A few reference grammars are eminently readable. Christo van der Merwe's *A Biblical Hebrew Reference Grammar*[31] is probably the most up-to-date, user-friendly, and readable grammar of them all. Explanations are clear and concise. Chapters are well structured. Examples are numerous, and all examples are glossed.

Another grammar suitable for reading and review is Bill T. Arnold and John H. Choi's *A Guide to Biblical Hebrew Syntax*.[32] The volume is "intended to introduce basic and critical issues of Hebrew syntax to beginning and intermediate students."[33] Each chapter delves into a particular syntactic category. An opening paragraph defines the grammatical concept. Examples of common exegetical uses follow, complete with pointed Hebrew text and translation.

Bruce K. Waltke and Michael O'Connor's *An Introduction to Biblical Hebrew Syntax*,[34] referenced in both van der Merwe and in Arnold and Choi, should also be included in our discussion of readable grammars. Although these three grammars have characteristically been used for reference, one who has a desire to maintain an understanding of Hebrew for the long haul will benefit tremendously from time spent in one or more of these great resources.

Summaries of Hebrew syntax also serve the lifelong learner of Hebrew well. Robert Chisholm's *From Exegesis to Exposition: A Practical Guide to Using Biblical Hebrew*, while pointing the way to moving from text to sermon, also provides a very helpful summary and review of Hebrew semantics and syntax in chapters 4–6.[35]

One other very helpful work deserves mention before moving on to a discussion of text-focused strategies. Susan Anne

Groom's *Linguistic Analysis of Biblical Hebrew*[36] is an informed, lucidly written introduction to the use of linguistic methods for the study of the Hebrew text of the Old Testament. Particularly important for our purposes are her chapters on "Lexical Semantics" and "Text Linguistics." Groom's writing is admirably clear, her work is insightful and practical, and her many Hebrew examples are well chosen and translated into English. Although her *Linguistic Analysis of Biblical Hebrew* is not a Hebrew reference grammar, her in-depth linguistic analysis of the language is an important resource that addresses the problem of meaning in Hebrew.

Suggested Strategy: It is important that you read at the pace of comprehension. The goal of this aspect of reacquaintance with the reference literature of biblical Hebrew is very much in keeping with the stated aim of van der Merwe's *Grammar* "to serve as *a reference work at an intermediate level* for exegetes and translators of the Hebrew Bible who have a basic knowledge of biblical Hebrew, but would like to *use and broaden* the knowledge they have acquired in an introductory course."[37] Whether you would choose to read van der Merwe, Arnold and Choi, Waltke and O'Connor, Chisholm, or another grammar, the reading should not be rushed. Again, comprehension should determine the pace.

Having given consideration to keeping your Hebrew healthy by reviewing it, we will now consider how to keep your Hebrew healthy by using it.

Keeping Your Hebrew Healthy by Using It—Text-Focused Strategies

The most effective way to keep your Hebrew healthy is to *use it*. So far, the emphasis has been placed on review. Reviewing vocabulary and reviewing the fundamentals of Hebrew grammar and syntax both provide a solid foundation upon which to build. But keeping your Hebrew healthy requires that you use the language. Time spent immersed in the Hebrew text is the most effective way to maintain a working knowledge of the language. We will consider several strategies that incorporate techniques for a broad range of learning styles.

The Value of Listening to the Reading of the Hebrew Text

Since biblical Hebrew is taught as a literary language, there is little time given to and even less emphasis placed on reading Hebrew aloud and listening to the language as part of elementary Hebrew instruction. And yet, listening to the Hebrew language is one of the most fundamental and effective ways to learn it, to retain it, and to use it for lifelong ministry. Listening to a language is how we have all learned the language we speak. Listening to biblical Hebrew is a more natural experience than reading about it. Hearing the language is a more effective strategy for retaining it. Listening to the reading of biblical Hebrew enables one to internalize the language and to develop a listening comprehension of it.

Resources to facilitate a listening comprehension of biblical Hebrew are readily available. Programmed instructional readings, more limited in scope, provide a rich experience with the language that is both auditory and visual. Programmed instructional readings usually include an audio CD (or set of CDs) and a workbook. The audio CD contains Hebrew readings of selected biblical portions. The workbook provides a variety of reading assistance tools, such as vocabulary assistance, identification of nominal and verbal forms, and annotations on idioms and syntax. Readings of the canonical text, the other principal resource available, usually offer no lexical or grammatical assistance to the user, but the scope of readings is inclusive of all books of the Hebrew Bible. Both types of resources are invaluable for maintaining a working knowledge of biblical Hebrew.

Programmed Instructional Readings

Jessica W. Goldstein's *The First Hebrew Reader: Guided Selections from the Hebrew Bible*[38] comes with a companion audio CD and provides direct contact with biblical texts selected from a broad range of biblical genres. Each of the eighteen readings—

seven selected from the Law, four drawn from the Former and Latter Prophets, and seven from the Writings—provides a translation of the Hebrew text, a list of glossed vocabulary words from the passage, a verb analysis chart, and basic grammatical notes. The companion audio CD presents a reading of each passage and includes both male and female voices. The workbook and CD offer an excellent starting point for anyone desiring to jumpstart their Hebrew. The audio component in conjunction with the translation and annotations make it possible for anyone who has completed as little as one year of biblical Hebrew to pick up where he or she left off and to make rapid progress toward proficient use of the language.

Suggested Strategy: Approach one lesson at a time, not more than one lesson per day. For each listening session, proceed as follows: (1) Listen to the reading of the passage in Hebrew, following along with the Hebrew text provided at the top of the right page in *The First Hebrew Reader* workbook. (2) At the conclusion of the reading, note the New Vocabulary listed at the top of the left-hand page. (3) Review the Verb Analysis (parsings) chart provided in the middle of the left-hand page. (4) Read the Grammatical Notes at the bottom of the left page. (5) Now read aloud each clause of the Hebrew text. Use the Hebrew text provided in the lower half of the right-hand page of the workbook. After reading each clause, take note of the translation provided. Correlate what you have read in Hebrew with the translation provided. (6) Listen once again to the Hebrew reading. Follow along this time in your own copy of the Hebrew Bible. (7) Now, close your Hebrew Bible. Close your copy of *The First Hebrew Reader* and listen to the Hebrew reading of the passage one final time. Even if you do not understand all that you are hearing, you will understand some of it; and with each new lesson, you will understand more. You will hear familiar vocabulary. You will increasingly distinguish verbs from nouns and particles. You will recognize words and forms. You will deepen your understanding of syntax and structure. Hebrew will increasingly become a part of the way you think.

Randall Buth's *Living Biblical Hebrew* series, first developed in 1996 in Jerusalem, has proved to be a creative and effective program for Hebrew language acquisition and retention.[39] Buth draws from a broad spectrum of language teachers and theorists,[40] appropriating techniques that utilize listening comprehension and monolingual immersion. The printed and recorded instructional materials are designed to develop an "active knowledge" of biblical Hebrew. Both visual and auditory learners will benefit immediately from the picture lessons and recordings that constitute this approach. Buth's method offers the user a fresh, effective, and methodologically sound approach for developing linguistic competency in biblical Hebrew. Pastors and teachers will find his *Living Biblical Hebrew: Selected Readings with 500 Friends* a particularly valuable resource for sustained review of vocabulary, grammar and morphology, and pronunciation. The "500 Friends" are the most common words in the Hebrew Bible. Each word (noun, verb, particle) is glossed, the number of occurrences is listed, helpful derived forms are presented, and sample sentences from the Hebrew Bible are provided to give the word a context and to illustrate how the word is used. The biblical selections on the accompanying audio CD are read at a relaxed pace and include Genesis 1:1–2:3; Genesis 22; Exodus 19–20; Deuteronomy 6:4–9; Ruth 1–4; Psalms 8, 23, 150; and Proverbs 3:1–8. The final section, titled "The Hebrew Verb: A Short Syntax," provides a more detailed and technical discussion of the tense-aspect system, volitional structures, word order, the sequential tense system, nonsequential word order, and special poetic use of the tense-aspects.

Readings of the Canonical Text

Hearing the Hebrew Bible read is indispensable if you are going to maintain a working knowledge of the language. Listening to the language will reinforce and give coherence to all other facets of Hebrew language study, because hearing the language provides the missing ingredient to all other aspects of study, namely, context. Hearing vocabulary words, verb forms, and clause sequences is vital to the long-term health of one's Hebrew. Listening to the reading of a chapter from the Hebrew Bible, or even better, listening to the reading of an entire book, has a benefit that cannot be replicated by any other form of study. The ears will hear what the eyes cannot see! The grammatical forms and sounds of the language, combining in the most natural way as an act of communication, yield insight and understanding of the Hebrew Scriptures that cannot otherwise be gained.

Readings of the full canonical text are obtainable and affordable. *The Hebrew Bible Narrated*[41] provides an excellent, high-quality recording of the Hebrew Scriptures originally broadcast on Israel National Television and radio stations, one chapter every night. The set contains four audio CDs (MP3 format) and covers all books of the Hebrew Canon. The entire Hebrew Bible is also available in MP3–CD format through Audio Scriptures International.[42]

Suggested Strategy: Begin your effort to maintain your Hebrew with an audio resource that provides both auditory and visual assistance. Jessica Goldstein's *The First Hebrew Reader* and Randall Buth's *Living Biblical Hebrew* series are both user-friendly, helpful, informative, and ideal for revitalizing Hebrew language study for lifelong use. Proceed one lesson at a time, not more than one lesson or unit per day. Allow what you have heard and read to settle and find its place in your broader understanding of the language. When you have completed the lessons in one, or both, of these resources, you are ready to begin to listen to more extended readings of the Hebrew Scriptures. Here I will suggest reading along two different tracks, one canonical, and the other pragmatic. On the canonical track, you will begin to make your way through the Hebrew Bible. On the pragmatic track, you will begin to focus on selected passages that are of more immediate importance to you and your preaching or teaching ministry.

Although you may choose to begin with any narrative portion, it is beneficial to start at the beginning! Maintain a pace of one chapter each day, or if you desire, one chapter every other day. Listen to the Hebrew reading of the chapter completely through. As you listen, you will hear words and forms and structures with which you are familiar. You will recognize vocabulary words and verb forms, and you will understand phrases and sometimes clauses and entire verses. Do not worry about words and forms you do not know. Those words and forms will come with time and a commitment to grow your vocabulary long-term. After you have heard the entire chapter, turn to the passage in a standard English version, like the New International Version, New American Standard Version, New Revised Standard Version, English Standard Version, or New Jewish Version, and read the entire passage aloud. The reading in English will give clarity and cohesiveness to your understanding of what is happening in the chapter as a whole. Now, return to the recorded Hebrew reading, and listen once again to the Hebrew reading of the chapter in its entirety. Continue on this pace until you have read each chapter of the Hebrew Bible.

On a reading track of more immediate benefit to you, allow your projected preaching and teaching schedule to determine which Old Testament passages or biblical books you will listen to. Listening to the Hebrew text is one of the best-kept secrets of Hebrew exegesis. Months in advance of pulpit exposition, even years in advance of close exegetical study, one can listen to the reading of the Hebrew text of portions of Scripture that are slated for exposition. Far in advance of detailed textual analysis, you can begin to experience the world of the text—the sounds, the rhythms—and gain great benefit from hearing the story or the poem unencumbered by translation.

The Value of Reading the Hebrew Text

The importance of reading the Hebrew text cannot be overstated. Although it is closely related to what we have just been discussing, reading the Hebrew text affects one differently than listening to it. Listening to the reading of the Hebrew text is a passive exercise. Reading the Hebrew text requires concentration and active engagement. Such increased attentiveness enables you to see things that you may not hear. Both listening and reading have their place in the study of biblical Hebrew. Both listening and reading are essential for maintaining the health of your Hebrew.

The reading of the Hebrew text should always be done aloud, if at all possible. Engaging both the eyes and the ears will maximize the benefit. The reading of meaningful literary units will facilitate comprehension. When one is reading Hebrew text for an understanding of the whole, the reading should be characterized by continuity. The reading should not be interrupted to make notes or even to look up the meaning of a word.

Read the Hebrew Text with the Assistance of a Parallel English Translation

This technique has been used with great success in Jewish education. The parallel column format of such a resource makes it ideally suited for any reader who is just beginning to read the text of the Hebrew Bible. Each page has two columns. The right column presents the biblical Hebrew text broken down phrase by phrase (usually five to six verses per page). The parallel left column offers a phrase-by-phrase English translation that corresponds fully to the Hebrew text in the right column. This arrangement facilitates the direction of writing for both languages and makes it possible for the user to have ready access to English glosses for Hebrew vocabularies that have not yet been learned or mastered. The parallel column format differs from the more traditional interlinear layout in that the Hebrew text is not interspersed with English. This is a definite advantage for developing competency in reading Hebrew. If an English translation or gloss is placed right below the Hebrew text, the eye will naturally gravitate to the English and, inadvertently, will develop a dependency on the presence of English. In the parallel column format, although the English translation column is available, it is removed from the Hebrew text. The translation on the left side of the page can be covered up, so all that the eye sees is the Hebrew text. The English translation is readily available, if needed, but the Hebrew text remains the focus.

Rabbi Pesach Goldberg's *Linear Chumash* covers the five books of the Pentateuch.[43] Each of the five volumes (totaling 1,252 pages) gives a word for word translation of the phrase-by-phrase breakdown of the Hebrew text. Although Goldberg's translation is based entirely upon Rashi's commentary, the translation is fairly literal, accurate, and easy to track with the Hebrew text. Also available and similarly formatted is Goldberg's *Linear Megillos: Esther*.[44] These volumes have been effective tools in early Jewish learning, and they provide a rich resource for anyone desiring to build and maintain a reading knowledge of Hebrew. Reading one page, as few as five to six verses a day, in resources such as these provides three-and-a-half years of readings in the Hebrew text of the Pentateuch. This approach to reading the Hebrew text—phrase by phrase, clause by clause—reinforces learned vocabulary, introduces the reader to new words in context, and trains the eye to work with the basic syntactical units of the language. The linear format makes reading manageable, more enjoyable, and prepares the reader for navigating longer passages.

Read a Verse or Two from the Hebrew Text as a Vital Part of your Devotional Time

Reading the Hebrew text can be a spiritual discipline of great benefit. Another approach to reading the Hebrew text provides for the identification of key forms and glosses but does not offer a translation of the Hebrew text. The verses can, of course, be those of your own choosing. However, pre-selected readings are available. The volumes edited by Heinrich Bitzer and David W. Baker offer prepared readings for each day of the year from both the Hebrew Bible and the Greek New Testament. Each page of Heinrich Bitzer's two volumes provides, for every day of the year, a verse from the Hebrew text and a verse from the Greek text, which he intends to be read (aloud!) as a way of helping ministers and theologians retain the use of their biblical languages and grow in their knowledge of the Scriptures.[45] Throughout both volumes, Bitzer provides in footnote form glosses for Hebrew vocabulary as well as parsings for Hebrew verb forms. Glosses are not provided for the Greek text, because the authors assume that readers will have greater familiarity with the Greek.

The volume by David W. Baker and Elaine A. Heath, *More Light on the Path*,[46] follows the same format as Bitzer's work. For each of the 365 days of the year, Hebrew and Greek readings are provided, along with glosses for Hebrew vocabulary and parsings for Hebrew verb forms. Additionally, Baker provides glosses and parsings for the Greek text, as well as a brief prayer or devotional thought based on the readings for the day.

Bitzer's overriding concern is expressed in his preface. He writes, "The more a theologian detaches himself from the basic Hebrew and Greek text of Holy Scripture, the more he detaches himself from the source of real theology!"[47] Could we not paraphrase Heinrich Bitzer by saying, "The more a pastor or teacher detaches himself from the basic Hebrew and Greek text of Holy Scripture, the more he detaches himself from the very word he is to proclaim!" Even the modest reading of a verse a day from the Hebrew text will go a long way in preserving a working knowledge of biblical Hebrew.

Read the Hebrew Text with Others Who Have Studied Biblical Hebrew

Although reading the Hebrew text will usually be done alone, reading Hebrew with others is of great benefit. Inquire of pastors and students in the area. Form a Hebrew reading group for mutual support and instruction. The value of personal, private reading of Hebrew can easily be offset by a sense of solitude and aloneness in such an endeavor. Much can be gained, and a reading knowledge of the language can more easily be maintained, by reading the Hebrew text with others. The common goal of maintaining your Hebrew, the mutual support that a reading group provides, and the shared accountability of following through on a commitment makes reading the Hebrew text with others tremendously beneficial.

I occasionally hear of seminary graduates and local pastors who have formed a small group that meets once each week to read the Hebrew Bible together. All members of the reading group have studied Hebrew at some point in a seminary or university. All participants desire to maintain a reading knowledge of Hebrew and not to lose what they worked so hard for. Every one of them is convinced of the value of maintaining a working knowledge of the language. All of them are fully committed to upholding each other in their desire to grow in their understanding of Hebrew and to using the language effectively in their respective ministries. And so they meet each week to read—to read Isaiah, to read through the Psalms, to read through the Pentateuch. They read together, and they encourage each other in their reading.

Always Use the Hebrew Text in Preparation for Preaching and Teaching

Seize every opportunity to use your Hebrew. Make use of the language your default. Whether you are exegeting the text for a future sermon series or preparing a devotional for a prayer breakfast, use the Hebrew text in your preparation. This very simple, practical step is one of the most important factors, perhaps *the* most important factor, in keeping your Hebrew healthy. If you have been called to communicate to people what God has said, then you need to *know* exactly what God has said! What God has said is given to us in his Word, and it was given in the language of the Canaanite marketplace. Although centuries of translations have made that word available and understandable to generations, a translation—even a translation that strives to be faithful to the original—is still a translation. It is always one step removed. It offers a restricted view. It is a rendering of the original that is subject to source and target language constraints. The one whom God has chosen to declare his Word must be able to know what God has said without restrictions. What is required to fulfill that calling is unfiltered access to what God has revealed in his Word. A vital working knowledge of Hebrew makes possible unfiltered access.

Analyzing the Hebrew text of Scripture is fundamentally detective work. Exegetical study requires the ability to observe what is there, noting clues found in the structure and semantic contours of the text, and then drawing conclusions that yield an interpretation. Everything in the text matters! Every word is important. Every structure reflects a choice that an author has made. Nothing is superfluous. Every component of the text has its function. Knowing how to navigate the Hebrew text by reading and understanding what is actually there makes the difference, at least for a pastor, between preaching the text and preaching the translation. As we have already noted, translators make hundreds of decisions, many of which affect the interpretation of a passage. If the only access one has to the biblical text is through a translation, what does one do where the translations differ?

The most reliable guide we have to what God has said in the first thirty-nine books of the Bible is the Hebrew text of Scripture. One of the keys to maintaining the health of your Hebrew is to use the language every opportunity you have. If a knowledge of biblical Hebrew is exercised on a regular basis, especially if it is daily, then your Hebrew will not only remain healthy, but your knowledge of the language will increase, and with that increase will come greater understanding of what God has said to us. Several resources make access to the text and analysis of it more available, more feasible than at any other time in history. Pastors and teachers who have had as little as one year of Hebrew now have every reason and no shortage of resources to help maintain and develop their competency in biblical Hebrew.

Try Computer-Assisted Biblical Study

Some claim that "technology has changed everything." Fortunately, technology has not changed *everything*, but technology has changed many things. It has certainly changed how Hebrew can be taught, and it has changed immeasurably how Hebrew can be used effectively by pastors and teachers for the ministry of the Word. The use of electronic text and software has revolutionized biblical studies. Technology has made it possible for the exegete to examine more of the Hebrew text than was previously possible, and technology has made it possible for the exegete to work more accurately in the text than ever before. Details of the text are instantly accessible, and the corpus in which one is working is now manageable. All occurrences of a word in any form can be retrieved in a matter of seconds, whether from within a particular book, or corpus, or the entire Canon. Collocations, or specific combinations of words, can be searched for analysis within seconds. Verb forms and sequences and syntactical structures can be collected and studied and understood with greater clarity and confidence than was previously possible—all of this making for unparalleled precision, clarity, and transparency in preaching.

Two original language software resources make it possible to use Hebrew efficiently and effectively. Both *Gramcord*[48] and *BibleWorks*[49] provide powerful platforms for nuanced, detailed grammatical study of the Hebrew text. Difficult forms cannot pose an obstacle to one's study because *Gramcord* and *BibleWorks* provide morphological identifications and lexical definitions for Hebrew words by simply passing the cursor over words in the displayed Hebrew text. Grammatical and syntactical searches, the "bread and butter" of exegesis and exposition, can be simple or complex. A search can be performed on a particular word (lemma), or word combination (order specific), or string of words (phrase or clause). The search can be based solely on a lexeme distributed over several chapters or books, or the search can be morphologically specific and context sensitive. Both *Gramcord* and *BibleWorks* are easy to use and both are reasonably priced. Both programs make accessible the kind of textual information needed for accurate and comprehensible teaching and preaching. *Gramcord* and *BibleWorks* provide a doorway to discoveries in the Hebrew text that is limited only by the inquisitiveness of the exegete.

Several Hebrew lexicons are now available in electronic format. *The New Brown-Driver-Briggs Hebrew and English Lexicon (Complete and Unabridged Electronic Edition)* is available from Varda Books.[50] This 2004 Scholar PDF edition is "a searchable, electronic replica of the printed original prepared in Adobe PDF format, complete with sophisticated, high-quality navigation capability."[51] Also available in electronic format (CD-ROM edition) is *The Hebrew and Aramaic Lexicon of the Old Testament*.[52]

Other Resources

Other resources facilitate working in the Hebrew text as well. Frederic Putnam's *A Cumulative Index to the Grammar and Syntax of Biblical Hebrew*[53] provides access by way of a verse-by-verse index to fourteen introductory, intermediate, and advanced grammars of biblical Hebrew, such as Gesenius-Kautzsch-Cowley, Waltke and O'Connor, Gibson, Williams, Bauer and Leander, Bergsträsser, Joüon-Muraoka, and others. This is a valuable reference tool regardless of where in the Canon one is working. A quick check of the index will indicate where the grammar and syntax of one's passage is referred to or discussed in the standard grammars of biblical Hebrew.

Conclusion

Learning biblical Hebrew is a great privilege. Keeping your Hebrew healthy makes it possible to reap the benefits of knowing the language. You find you are able to check the accuracy and reliability of modern translations and paraphrases. You can now identify the reason for translational divergence and evaluate more fairly the spectrum of renderings. You can assess with greater confidence and discernment the comments and observations of commentators. Your understanding of Hebrew positions you to discover the structure and rhetorical techniques of the Old Testament writers that are often lost or obscured in translation. Use of the language enables you to unravel complicated grammatical structures and begin to understand otherwise enigmatic forms of expression. You find that the application of language skills acquired equips you to clarify otherwise problematical and perplexing portions of the Old Testament Scriptures. You can now illustrate or illumine a doctrine or truth by means of a Hebrew word or semantic field study. Knowledge of Hebrew opens new avenues for teaching and preaching from the first thirty-nine books of the Bible. You realize that your Hebrew study has broadened and enriched your perspective on the ancient Near East, and the land and people of the Bible. But perhaps most rewarding, having persevered in your Hebrew study, you begin to experience the joy of seeing those under your spiritual care grow and flourish in their understanding of and love for the Old Testament.

Keeping your Hebrew healthy is, indeed, possible. By periodically reviewing and daily using it, you can maintain a working knowledge of Hebrew that will manifest itself by clear and compelling exposition. The opportunity to study Hebrew was a gift. The responsibility to use what you have learned and to keep your Hebrew healthy is a stewardship.

Questions to Consider

1. Why do you think maintaining one's facility with biblical Hebrew is important?
2. What kind of learner are you?
3. How can you develop a plan for practicing your Hebrew?
4. What's your plan?

On the Shelf

Baker, David W. and Elaine A. Heath [with Morven R. Baker]. *More Light on the Path*. Grand Rapids: Baker, 1998.

Bitzer, Heinrich, ed. *Light on the Path: Daily Scripture Readings in Hebrew and Greek*, vol. 2. Marburg: Oekumenischer Verlag, Dr. R. F. Edel, 1973.

Chisholm, Robert B., Jr. *From Exegesis to Exposition: A Practical Guide to Using Biblical Hebrew*. Grand Rapids: Baker, 1998.

Van Pelt, Miles V. *Old Testament Hebrew Vocabulary Cards*. Grand Rapids: Zondervan, 2003.

Van Pelt, Miles V. and Gary D. Pratico. *The Vocabulary Guide to Biblical Hebrew*. Grand Rapids: Zondervan, 2003.

3

Preaching from the Historical Books

Carol M. Kaminski

The historical books of the Old Testament cover the period beginning with the conquest of the land under Joshua and continue until the Persian Period in the fifth century BC. Twelve books are included under the designation *historical*: Joshua, Judges, Ruth, 1 and 2 Samuel, 1 and 2 Kings, 1 and 2 Chronicles, Ezra, Nehemiah, and Esther.[1] Within this section of the Canon, some books are evidently more popular in churches than others. Nehemiah, for example, provides great subject matter for a preaching series, but what about other books, such as Kings or Chronicles? When was the last time you preached a series on the southern kingdom? Even the *thought* of preaching on the historical books raises the question: how does one apply these stories to *our* context today? The historical books undoubtedly present challenges for the pastor who seeks to bridge the gap between an ancient text and the church today. Some regrettably neglect preaching from these books since the gap seems insurmountable. But if we affirm that the *whole* counsel of God is to be preached and that *all* Scripture is profitable, we may well ask whether there is a way of preaching from these books that is both engaging and relevant to twenty-first-century Christians.

The Bible Is *One* Redemptive Story

There has been an increasing awareness among scholars and lay persons alike of the importance of seeing the Bible as *story*. That is, instead of seeing the Bible as a compilation of isolated or disconnected parts, it is a book that tells *one* unified story of God's redemptive plan for humanity, beginning with Israel, but for the sake of the world. This larger narrative provides coherence to the various sections of the Old Testament by underscoring that each individual book contributes to the broader redemptive story. There is, therefore, one metanarrative to which the individual stories belong.

But do laypeople in the church actually *know* this narrative? Does it inform their choices and the way they live? People delight in Tolkien's Lord of the Rings, and in Lewis's Chronicles of Narnia, but how many church folk fully grasp that the Bible tells *one* unified story and that its missionary thrust is intended to shape our communities? If the Old Testament is deemed to be irrelevant and too difficult to understand, which is sadly often the case, God's story cannot be fully known. As a consequence, our lives will be more informed and shaped by the culture than the biblical story. There is a great need in the church, therefore, for pastors to help their congregations understand how the individual stories in the Old Testament contribute to the larger redemptive plan of God. It is essential that Christians understand the "big picture" of the biblical story so that they can fully grasp what God was doing *then*, and how the church is to continue God's missional work in the world *now*. More recent emphasis on the Bible as *story* reminds us, therefore, that the historical books are not simply a collection of antiquated stories that are irrelevant for the church today.

Nor are they a compilation of stories whose primary value is to teach ethical or moral principles. To be sure, the Old Testament is dynamic and multifaceted since it entails God's covenantal relationship with Israel, but the individual books tell *one* story of the outworking of God's redemptive plan for humanity.[2]

Although the historical books are designated "historical," the term is somewhat misleading since these books are not simply narrating history—they are telling a *theological* story that is communicated through narrative.[3] The challenge for the pastor, then, is to know how to preach a sermon from the historical books that is both sensitive to the theological import of the story and relevant to twenty-first-century Christians. One may well ask whether there are some hermeneutical principles that can inform the pastor when preparing a sermon from these books. If the Old Testament tells *one* redemptive story, how does this influence how preachers prepare sermons from the historical books and how they apply it today?

Preaching the Historical Books Theologically

When preparing a sermon on the historical books, it is important that the passage be located in its literary context and interpreted in light of the larger redemptive narrative. But what difference does this *really* make for a sermon? We are all familiar with the story of Jericho, when the walls fall down under the leadership of Joshua (Joshua 6). But how would you *apply* this story in your congregation today? Is it in any way relevant to the people in your church?

The Story of Jericho

If you interpret the falling down of Jericho's walls *without* the larger redemptive narrative in view, you might conclude that the main idea of the story is *faith*. As a pastor, you might encourage your congregation to live by faith, following the example of Joshua. This emphasis on faith could also be affirmed by citing Hebrews 11, which says, "By faith the walls of Jericho fell, after the people had marched around them for seven days" (Heb. 11:30). Some of you may be even more *specific*, exhorting your congregation to trust God for the "walls" that they are facing. These "walls" could be any number of things, such as job loss, financial crises, sickness, or family problems. Joshua faced "impossible" circumstances, but they were overcome by faith. So, too, Christians are to trust that God would break down *their* obstacles. Since everybody faces difficulties at one time or another, this has the potential to be a great sermon. But is this really the main idea of the story? What difference would it make if this passage were interpreted with the larger redemptive story in view?

In the immediate literary context of the book, we learn that Joshua had already sent two men to spy out Jericho (Joshua 2). They return with a positive report, affirming that God has, indeed, given them the land (Josh. 2:24). Now in our passage, God tells Joshua that he has given Jericho into *Joshua's* hand (Josh. 6:1–5). As Joshua leads the people around the city, doing exactly what God has told him, the walls of Jericho fall down (Josh. 6:20–21). God is using somewhat "unusual" circumstances (that require faith) to bring to fruition his promise to *Joshua*.

But this story is also to be interpreted *theologically* as part of the larger narrative: God had promised Abraham, Isaac, and Jacob that he would give them the land of Canaan.[4] This promise, which is subsequently taken up by Israel, is a major theme of Deuteronomy as Moses prepares the new generation on the plains of Moab to enter the land. And as Moses's newly appointed successor, Joshua is to lead the conquest. If the defeat of Jericho is interpreted with this larger narrative in view, the walls of Jericho fall down because God is fulfilling his promise of land made to Abraham hundreds of years earlier. It reminds us, therefore, about the character of God, that he is faithful and able to bring about what he has promised. The faithfulness of God is *exactly* what Joshua reflects upon when he speaks to the Israelites prior to his death:

> Now I am about to go the way of all the earth. You know with all your heart and soul that not one of all the good promises the Lord your God gave you has failed. Every promise has been fulfilled; not one has failed.
>
> Joshua 23:14

While the walls of Jericho do fall down, God is *not* promising that *our* "walls" will fall down—nor is there any indication in the text to suggest that we *ought* to apply the story to ourselves in this way. First, this exegetical fallacy, called *personalizing*, assumes that the main point of the story is its application to *us*. Second, this way of applying the story entails *allegorizing*, that is, it interprets the "literal" walls of Jericho in an allegorical way to correlate with *our* obstacles. But the story was never intended to be interpreted in this way. The danger of this approach is that it assumes that God is promising *us* something when he is not. This can cause problems pastorally: What if my obstacles do not fall down? Does this mean that God is unfaithful or that my lack of faith is the problem? The central issue is that this type of allegorical application is based on a faulty methodology that interprets the story in isolation from the larger redemptive context and assumes that there is a "deeper" meaning in the text. Another example of allegorizing is the story of David and Goliath, which is commonly interpreted to mean that Christians are to face the "giants" in their own lives. Such an application again fails to interpret the story within the larger redemptive narrative, and it assumes that the "giants" we face are analogous to Goliath!

While the story of Jericho clearly underscores the importance of faith, it is ultimately a story about God and *his* faithfulness. We can affirm that the God who was faithful to Joshua—and to the patriarchs—is *our* God. He can be trusted for he has shown himself over and over again to be faithful. The stories of the Old Testament teach us about the character of God and the way he is working out his redemptive plan—for the God of the Old Testament is none other than the Lord *our* God.

The Story of Rehoboam

The importance of keeping the larger redemptive narrative in view may be seen by looking at another story recorded in the historical books in 1 Kings 12. After the death of King Solomon, his son Rehoboam becomes king. All the people of Israel gather before him, asking him to lighten their load after many years of hard service under his father. Rehoboam consults the elders, who tell him to listen to the request of the people. But he rejects their counsel and listens to the advice of the young men, who tell him to increase the workload of the people. This leads to civil war, ushering in the period of the divided monarchy. But how is a preacher to *apply* this passage to a twenty-first-century congregation?

If this story is interpreted *without* the larger narrative in view, a pastor might conclude that the main idea is that it shows what can go wrong when a leader does not listen to the advice of elders. Rehoboam rejected the wise counsel given by his elders and everything fell apart. So the moral principle is that Christians should listen to the wisdom of elders within their church community. This exegetical fallacy, called *moralizing*, assumes that the main point of the Old Testament story is to teach a moral principle. There is even the inherent danger of preaching "biblical" principles from the wrong text if the larger context is not the guiding hermeneutic. In this text, the question is not whether there is wisdom in listening to elders—for one would agree that this is generally a good biblical principle—but whether it is the main point of *this* story.

If one considers the *literary* context, the division of the kingdom is preceded by the story about Rehoboam's father Solomon, who married foreign women and served their gods (1 Kings 11:1–8). Solomon had not kept God's covenant, so God told him that the kingdom would be torn away from him. Yet because of David, God would not bring about this judgment during Solomon's lifetime; he would tear the kingdom away from Solomon's *son* (1 Kings 11:11–12). God then told Jeroboam through a prophet that *Jeroboam* would be the leader of the ten tribes (1 Kings 11:28–39). This is the background against which Rehoboam's actions, which led to the division of the kingdom, are to be interpreted.

After Rehoboam had increased the workload of the people, the following summary is given: "So the king did not listen to the people, for this turn of events was from the Lord, to fulfill the word the Lord had spoken to Jeroboam son of Nebat through Ahijah the Shilonite" (1 Kings 12:15). It is important to observe that the narrator does not give a "moral principle" at the conclusion of the story, which could indicate that the moral principle is central to the narrative. Rather, the narrator reminds the reader that what took place was in fulfillment of the prophetic word to Jeroboam. This is because the division of the kingdom is being interpreted *within* the narrative, not as an isolated story that teaches a moral principle.

This is, indeed, one of the challenges when preaching from the historical books since it is easy to find a "moral principle" from the Old Testament that can be applied in a church setting. It is more difficult and time intensive, however, to consider the significance of the story *theologically* in the context of the larger narrative. In the case of Rehoboam's actions, the story shows how God's judgment against Solomon came to pass and underscores God's providence in the seemingly "human" events. But there is also the theme of God's mercy underlying the narrative, not only in this context, but throughout the book of Kings. According to the laws of the Mosaic covenant,[5] idolatry was a grave offense. The Israelites were repeatedly warned against making and worshiping idols; such covenant unfaithfulness would surely invoke God's wrath.[6] Even though Solomon worshiped many gods and had not kept God's covenant, God did *not* cut off Solomon or his kingdom. Rather, he showed him mercy for the sake of David (1 Kings 11: 34). God's judgment would surely fall upon his son Rehoboam, as seen in the division of the kingdom, but God did not fully take away Rehoboam's kingdom either, "for the sake of David" (1 Kings 11:13). So the kingdom was divided, but the fact that there even *was* a southern kingdom with such idolatrous kings testifies to the mercy of God.

In our churches today, the God of the Old Testament is too often seen to be legalistic and unforgiving. But the story of Rehoboam, when read in its narrative context, teaches us about the mercy of God, seen in his faithfulness to bring about his promise to David in spite of Solomon's idolatrous actions. (Rehoboam will not be any better!) When the southern kingdom comes to an end in 586 BC, for a brief moment God removes his compassion, but his mercy will not be fully exhausted. After the repeated failure of Judah's kings, and after a time of waiting, a righteous "Son of David" will be born in Bethlehem who will reign on David's throne (Luke 1:32–33). This is, indeed, an act of divine mercy (Luke 1:68–79).

The Historical Books Contribute to the Larger Redemptive Story

So within the larger narrative of the Bible, the historical books have an essential role to play. How can a congregation marvel at the coming of the righteous Son of David if they are not familiar with the failures of the Davidic kings who ruled *before* him? How can they understand the depth of God's compassion and mercy if they have not grappled with Israel's rebellious and stubborn heart? How can your congregation fully grasp the extent of Israel's idolatry, and indeed, the plight of humanity, *without* the books of Judges and Kings? While the law is given during the time of Moses, it is the *historical* books—books such as Judges, Samuel, Kings, and Chronicles—that show whether or not the Israelites actually *obeyed* God's laws. It is the historical books that reveal the character of God, and *our* sinful nature, which is exposed so powerfully in the story of Israel.

The historical books are, therefore, foundational for our understanding of God's redemptive story in the Bible, recording events that take place within *three* major periods of the Old Testament: the conquest of the land, the monarchy, and the return to Jerusalem. If we consider the Old Testament narrative, we can distinguish several periods, beginning with creation and continuing until the return from exile and rebuilding of the temple. These periods are highlighted on the following chart:

Creation and Fall	Abrahamic Promises	Exodus and Law	Conquest of Land	Monarchy	Exile to Babylon	Return to Jerusalem
Genesis 1–11	Genesis 12–50	Exodus Leviticus Numbers Deuteronomy	Joshua Judges Ruth	1–2 Samuel 1–2 Kings 1–2 Chronicles Prophets	2 Kings 25 2 Chronicles 36 Ezekiel Daniel	Ezra Nehemiah Esther Prophets

These few hundred years of history recorded in the historical books are central to our understanding of *the* story. But we do well to remember that these stories apply *first* to Israel and that their theological significance within the larger redemptive narrative needs to be fully grasped if we are to understand how they relate to *us* today. This will safeguard us from viewing them merely as isolated stories that apply primarily to us or as stories whose main point is to teach a moral principle—they are much more than this.

Preaching the Stories from a *Historical* Perspective

There is yet another challenge for the pastor when preparing sermons from the historical books. Recent emphasis on the Bible as *story* means, at times, that less priority is given to historical concerns. This can affect how one both approaches the historical books and preaches from them—for we all know that "historical information" is not what makes a good story. If the historical books contain stories about Israel, and if they are to be interpreted theologically as part of the metanarrative of the Bible, the question may well be raised, then, whether it is even *necessary* to include historical details in a sermon. What difference does it make?

Historical Information

Now consider the story of Hezekiah in 2 Chronicles 32.[7] During Hezekiah's reign, the Assyrians had been exerting pressure on Judah. The story takes a new turn, however, when Hezekiah rebels against Sennacherib; this is what happens:

> Later, when Sennacherib king of Assyria and all his forces were laying siege to Lachish, he sent his officers to Jerusalem with this message for Hezekiah king of Judah and for all the people of Judah who were there:
>
> "This is what Sennacherib king of Assyria says: On what are you basing your confidence, that you remain in Jerusalem under siege?"
>
> 2 Chronicles 32:9–10

The Assyrian messengers are intent on intimidating the people of Judah—they even tell the men who are defending the city walls that they will soon "eat their own filth and drink their own urine" (2 Kings 18:27). So they taunt those who are protecting the city, reminding them what the Assyrians have done to *other* nations, and assert that *their* God is unable to deliver them.

When preparing a sermon from the historical books, additional information can often be found about key individuals, peoples, places, and events in your text.[8] In our passage we can identify the following:

- Key *individuals*: Hezekiah, Sennacherib, and the messengers
- Key *peoples*: the Assyrians and the people of Judah
- Key *places*: Jerusalem and Lachish
- Key *events*: the battle of Lachish and Sennacherib's attack on Jerusalem

If you were able to find out additional information about the battle of Lachish, for example, what difference would it make for your sermon? Would it enhance your sermon or would "historical details" have the potential to ruin it?

The Battle of Lachish

The battle of Lachish is well attested in the archaeological record and in ancient Assyrian texts. We know from excavations that Lachish was a well-fortified city of Judah during the time of Hezekiah. But these heavy fortifications would not protect the city from the Assyrian army. Stone wall carvings over fifty feet long, known as the *Lachish Reliefs*, vividly depict the conquest of Lachish: siege engines batter the walls; infantry storm the city; women and their children are taken as plunder; three prisoners are stripped naked and impaled on stakes; and two captives are being flayed alive—this is unquestionably a cruel scene.[9] Excavations at Tel Lachish uncovered hundreds of iron arrowheads, slingstones, and a massive grave with dismembered skulls in one area. Sennacherib's assault on Judah is also recorded in an Assyrian text; here is an excerpt:

> I laid siege to 46 of his [Hezekiah's] strong cities, walled forts and to the countless small villages in their vicinity, and conquered (them) by means of well-stamped (earth-) ramps, and battering-rams brought (thus) near (to the walls) (combined with) the attack by foot soldiers.[10]

These ancient records are a stark reminder of how the Assyrians treated their enemies, but they are more—they give us insight into the *historical* context for the story of Hezekiah. We now realize that the brief comment at the beginning of the story—that the Assyrian messengers had come from *Lachish*—is anything but incidental or inconsequential. This event, in fact, sets the scene for the entire story. Let's now consider the implications of historical information for preaching.

The Importance of Historical Research

Historical research is necessary when preparing a sermon on the historical books for several reasons. First, it helps the preacher enter the biblical world. As has been noted, there is a cultural and historical distance between the ancient text of the Old Testament and our church context today. Historical research enables a pastor to understand and identify with the ancient world so that the stories can be told from *their* worldview. For example, when Hezekiah hears that Sennacherib's messengers have arrived in Jerusalem, he tears his clothes and covers himself with sackcloth, for it is, indeed, a day of mourning. Your congregation will identify with Hezekiah's plight as you help them understand who Sennacherib is and the horrific battle being fought at Lachish. When you remind your congregation that just a few miles away the people of Judah are being assaulted, women and children are being taken as plunder, and prisoners are being flayed alive, they will begin to grapple with the depth of Hezekiah's faith, and perhaps even reflect on their own journey of faith. They will be confronted with a king who is trusting in God even though he and his people are facing imminent and potentially barbaric death at the hands of the Assyrians. No wonder we read that "Hezekiah trusted in the LORD, the God of Israel. There was no one like him among all the kings of Judah, either before him or after him" (2 Kings 18:5). So by doing the historical research, your congregation will identify with the characters and events in the Old Testament as you help them hear the stories in their original context.

Second, incorporating historical information into your sermon provides insight into the biblical world for your congregation that would otherwise not be known, and they may even be interested to see pictures of the battle of Lachish or Sennacherib! Many Christians, however, have little knowledge of the rich archaeological data that furnishes the biblical text. These historical "insights" can make the stories come alive as your congregation learns new things about characters and events in the Bible that have been preserved in ancient inscriptions and in the archaeological record.

Third, there is a pervasive view in the culture which says that the Bible is not historically reliable. The Old Testament is thought to contain stories about the origins of Jews and

Christians, but they are oftentimes perceived to be *fictional*. Including historical details in your sermon provides a wonderful opportunity for you to remind your congregation that the people and events mentioned in the Old Testament *are* historical. In an age of skepticism, this positive view of the Bible can be a source of great encouragement.

Conclusion

We have suggested that the stories contained in the historical books need to be interpreted both *theologically* within the larger redemptive narrative and *historically* in the ancient world of the Old Testament. It has been stressed throughout this chapter that the historical books are not simply a collection of isolated or disconnected stories. Rather, the individual books contribute to the larger redemptive story, which begins with Israel, but is intended for the world. The historical books undoubtedly present challenges for the preacher, but these stories need to be preached if the church is to grasp the depth of the biblical story and its implications for how we live today. The culture provides many competing stories, but we need to be shaped and informed by God's story. Scripture implores us not to forget what God has done, yet many church folk do not even know the stories contained in the Old Testament. The historical books are often set aside, deemed too difficult, boring, or irrelevant. Since we are children of Abraham, these stories are, indeed, *our* stories, and we need to hear them afresh from pastors who are committed to preaching the *whole* counsel of God.

Questions to Consider

1. How does narrative function in communicating truth?
2. If the Old Testament tells *one* redemptive story, how does this influence how one prepares a sermon from the historical books and how one applies it today?

3. What is the value of incorporating historical research when preaching narratives?
4. Reflect on how you can take the tips from this chapter and put them into practice in your sermon preparation. What's your plan?

On the Shelf

Dictionaries and Encyclopedias

Buttrick, George A., ed. *The Interpreter's Dictionary of the Bible,* 4 vols. Nashville: Abingdon, 1962.

Bromiley, George W., ed. *The International Standard Bible Encyclopedia,* 4 vols. Grand Rapids: Eerdmans, 1979–1988.

Tenny, Merril C., ed. *The Zondervan Pictorial Encyclopedia of the Bible,* 5 vols. Grand Rapids: Zondervan, 1975.

History of the Old Testament

Arnold, Bill T., and Bryan E. Beyer. *Encountering the Old Testament.* Grand Rapids: Baker, 1999.

Bright, John. *A History of Israel,* 3rd ed. Philadelphia: Westminster, 1981.

Bruce, F. F. *Israel and the Nations: The History of Israel from the Exodus to the Fall of the Second Temple.* Revised by D. Payne. Downers Grove, IL: InterVarsity, 1997.

Dumbrell, William J. *The Faith of Israel: A Theological Survey of the Old Testament,* 2nd ed. Grand Rapids: Baker, 2002.

Kaiser, Walter C., Jr. *A History of Israel: From the Bronze Age through the Jewish Wars.* Nashville: Broadman & Holman, 1998.

Peoples of the Old Testament

Hoerth, Alfred J., Gerald L. Mattingly, and Edwin W. Yamauchi, eds. *Peoples of the Old Testament World.* Grand Rapids: Baker, 1994.

Wiseman, D. J., ed. *Peoples of Old Testament Times.* Oxford: Clarendon Press, 1973.

The Geography of the Old Testament

Aharoni, Yohanan, and Michael Avi-Yonah, ed. *The Macmillan Bible Atlas*, 3rd ed. New York: Macmillan, 1993.

The Archaeology of the Old Testament

Hoerth, Alfred J. *Archaeology and the Old Testament*. Grand Rapids: Baker, 1998.

Kaiser, Walter C., and Duane A. Garret, eds. *NIV Archaeological Study Bible*. Grand Rapids: Zondervan, 2005.

Mazar, A. *Archaeology of the Land of the Bible*. New York: Doubleday, 1990.

Pritchard, James B., ed. *Ancient Near Eastern Texts*. Princeton: Princeton University Press, 1969.

4

Preaching the Old Testament Narratives

Jeffrey D. Arthurs

Narrative is the largest genre of the Hebrew Bible. The Lord apparently values story, and we should too. Thankfully, that directive is not burdensome, because all people throughout all times have been storytellers. We depend on stories to make sense of the world. In the past twenty-five years, a remarkable consensus has formed among anthropologists, rhetoricians, sociologists, theologians, and others, that story is indispensable in embodying and transferring values. Performing all three of Cicero's functions of rhetoric, stories "prove," "delight," and "move."[1]

Therefore, because the Bible abounds in stories, because they are indispensable to human understanding, and simply because human beings love stories, we come to the subject of this chapter with delight: how can we prepare to preach Old Testament narratives? I contend that exegeting the text's literary features helps equip preachers to reproduce the text's rhetorical impact in their sermons. Paying attention to how the text communicates helps us understand how we can recommunicate. Before unfolding that thesis, four assertions provide some context for the argument.

First, I and the other authors of this volume believe that the Hebrew Bible, narrative portions included, is inspired by God and intended for our edification (2 Tim. 3:16). Since preachers speak on behalf of God, prayer must be part of our exegetical and homiletical "method." I will not emphasize that discipline in this chapter, but do not be misled by my silence.

Second, Old Testament narratives are theological. They reveal God. Sometimes Yahweh is the main "character" of the story, as in the creation account (Genesis 1–2); sometimes he enters and exits the scene, as in the story of the tower of Babel (Genesis 12); and sometimes he is absent, as in the book of Esther. But even when seemingly absent, he silently permeates every scene, moving events, judging deeds, and motivating the players through love or dread.

Third, concerning the thorny hermeneutical issue of preaching Christ from the Old Testament, I follow the perspective of biblical scholars Fee and Stuart: Hebrew narratives communicate truth on three levels.[2] The *top level* is the "macro-narrative," which portrays the creation and fall of humanity, the pervasive and universal effects of sin, and redemption through Messiah. The *middle level* traces the history of Israel: how God formed, blessed, watched, grieved over, disciplined, and restored the chosen people. The *bottom level* focuses on hundreds of individuals as examples of virtue and vice. Thus, working from the bottom up, any particular story may communicate principles for holy living, the record of God's chosen people, or an aspect of redemption history.[3]

Fourth, while Old Testament narratives are theological texts, they are more. They are also literary-rhetorical texts. They use a well-stocked tool chest of literary devices to influence beliefs, values, and actions. Persuasion comes by way of art, not argument. The following quotations from theologians and rhetoricians capture this aspect of Old Testament narratives:

> Holy Scripture is not a theoretical book of theological abstraction, but a book that intends to have a mighty influence on the lives of its readers.
>
> Bernard Ramm[4]

> The world of Scripture is not satisfied with claiming to be a historically true reality—it insists that it is the only real world. . . . The Scripture stories do not court our favor, they do not flatter us. . . . They seek to subject us, and if we refuse to be subjected, we are rebels.
>
> Eric Auerbach[5]

> The Bible's main form of exposition, the narrative, is most appropriately characterized as primary rhetoric, its primary objective being to persuade its audience.
>
> Dale Patrick and Allen Scult[6]

> A text is . . . an embodiment of an author's intention, that is a strategy designed to carry out that intention.
>
> John Sailhamer[7]

The rest of this chapter describes how to exegete and preach Hebrew narratives as literary-rhetorical texts by examining the genre's three key features: plot, character, and setting.

Plot

"Plot" is the causally linked chain of events in a story that moves a conflict from disequilibrium to resolution. Plot engages readers by inducing a feeling of suspense. We all want to know who "wins." This is the attention-sustaining power of a movie we are viewing for the first time.

However, even if we already know who "wins" because we are watching a rerun (which is the case with congregations "watching" many Old Testament narratives), plot still engages us by setting up and fulfilling expectations. For example, even though you know that Luke Skywalker "wins" by blowing up the Death Star, or that Jimmy Stewart's friends come to his aid on Christmas Eve, you might still enjoy watching classic films for the second, third, fourth, or even the ninth time! The attention-sustaining power of a rerun occurs in part because of the formal qualities of plot. While there is no suspense, there is still movement from disequilibrium to resolution, and audiences find that movement satisfying. Hearing an Old Testament narrative for the fourth time is like listening to the same piece of music four times. The satisfying experience of rhythm, dynamics, and chord progression is undiminished despite the lack of "suspense." In the same way, congregations can still be moved by the classic stories they have heard before: David and Goliath, Elijah on Mt. Carmel, crossing the Red Sea, and so forth. Indeed, congregations do request, "Tell me the old, old story."

Plots typically move from disequilibrium to resolution through five stages:

Background "Some time later God tested Abraham" (Gen. 22:1). Note, even this statement begins to create disequilibrium: God *tests* his friends?

Conflict "Take your son. . . . Sacrifice him" (Gen. 22:2). The disequilibrium smacks us with force.

Rising Action The journey to Moriah, Isaac carrying the wood, Isaac questioning his father ("Where is the lamb?"), Abraham building the altar, binding Isaac, preparing for sacrifice (Gen. 22:3–10).

Climax The angel stops Abraham (Gen. 22:11–12).

Resolution Abraham passes the test, God provides a ram for sacrifice, and God restates his covenant with Abraham (Gen. 22:13–19).

Old Testament narrative, like ancient narrative in general, emphasizes action more than character. Through plot, Old Testament authors *show* truth. That is, they communicate ideas obliquely by describing events, not by making assertions. They show ideas such as: God is sovereign (Esther), sinners who feel guilty try to hide their sin (David and Bathsheba), and God demands complete obedience (Saul and the Amalekites). Occasionally, narrators will interrupt their "showing" with "telling" (see Gen. 13:13; Gen. 29:18; 2 Sam. 6:8), but more typically they communicate ideas inductively, prompting the reader to infer the ideas as the story progresses. As narrative scholar Bar-Efrat states, "The plot serves to organize events in such a way as to arouse the reader's interest and emotional involvement, while at the same time imbuing the events with meaning."[8]

For example, the author of 1 Samuel 17 narrates the story of David and Goliath to communicate that God is mightier than the most intimidating champion his enemies can muster and that he blesses those who step out with fearless faith. Like a movie director determining what to show and how to show it, the author highlights these lessons through plot and point of view. The first two stages of the plot, background and conflict, begin with a close-up of Goliath, who appears as a technological and biological terror. His armor glistens, and his hulk dominates the field of battle. With a midrange shot, the camera shows the rising action: all Israel trembles; David, nearly defenseless, runs to Goliath; they exchange barbs; battle is joined. Then with slow motion the camera shows the climax: the big domino falls, and the resolution uses a wide angle to show the little dominoes collapsing in all directions. I do not have space in this short chapter to unfold more aspects of this skillful plot, but the next time you preach this text, ask yourself *how* the storyteller tells the story, and you will be better equipped to retell the story.

Literary-rhetorical analysis of plot contributes to homiletics in the following ways:

Choice of pericope: A homiletical truism states that preachers should preach thought units. Analysis of plot helps us do so. In narrative, a thought unit is a complete plot—background, conflict, rising action, climax, and resolution; or as Aristotle stated, a plot must have a beginning, middle, and end: "A well-constructed Plot . . . cannot either begin or end at any point one likes."[9] Dramatists and storytellers compose with scenes just as poets compose in strophes, and proverbialists compose with groups of short sayings. The impact a story makes on our minds and hearts does not usually result from individual words or lines. Rather, we remember scenes such as Odysseus escaping from the Cyclops; Huck lying to save Jim, the runaway slave; and Absalom hanging by his hair, pierced with three javelins.

Preaching texts from narrative literature are likely to be longer than preaching texts from epistles. Because it takes more time to show than to tell, the text of a sermon from narrative might be two or three chapters. With short stories like Ruth and Jonah, you may want to preach the entire book in one sermon. Don Sunukjian's sermon on the book of Esther is a model of how to preach the big idea of an entire plot.[10]

Big Idea: Since Old Testament narrators rarely spell out their theological or moral points, preachers who want to recommunicate as the text communicates should preach inductively. In inductive arrangement, the central idea of the sermon is stated only at the end, after the preacher has "embodied [the idea] in a structure of events and persons, rather than in a structure of verbal generalizations."[11] Narrative preachers can study with profit the induction of radio storyteller Paul Harvey who saves "the rest of the story" for the conclusion.[12]

Gifted preachers can even imply, rather than announce, the big idea. As homiletician Sidney Greidanus states, preaching from narrative should "be more suggestive than assertive."[13] Haddon Robinson echoes that opinion: "Narratives are most effective when the audience hears the story and arrives at the speaker's ideas without the ideas being stated directly. . . . Whether the points are stated or only implied depends on your skill as the preacher, the purpose of your sermon, and the awareness of the audience."[14]

Organization: Narrative form translates easily into homiletical form when we preach narrative sermons. Narrative-style preaching is a large and flexible net cast over many sermon forms. The key is to structure the sermon like the original plot, moving listeners from disequilibrium to resolution.

For example, the sermon can move from problem to solution, or it can move in causally linked scenes. The story can be narrated in the third person or first person. You can begin with a traditional introduction ("Today we're going to look at a story from ancient Israel . . ."), or you can plunge straight into the background and conflict ("His name was Jephthah. He was a judge. Not a judge in the fourth circuit court, but a judge in Israel, and he had a problem . . ."). You can end with a traditional conclusion ("We've seen how God rescues the meek. The next time you are in trouble . . ."), or you can simply end with the resolution of the story, prompting the audience to apply the truth to themselves so that they go away thinking, "I've got to be careful to. . . ."

As you retell the story, keep the plot moving with few interruptions. While you may need to pause briefly to explain cultural data or insert an aside, remember that much of the rhetorical force of narrative—suspense and engagement—lies in plot. Leverage the power the Lord has already put into the text.

The second key feature of narrative literature, character, has its own set of rhetorical and homiletical implications.

Character

"Character" is the depiction of the persons in a story, including all of their physical, psychological, social, and spiritual attributes. Old Testament stories, like all stories, center on the struggles of a protagonist, usually hindered or opposed by an antagonist. Supporting characters also appear, but exegetes will focus primarily on the protagonist and antagonist. The term "protagonist" means literally the "first" or "primary" struggler, and it reminds us that character cannot be separated from plot (except in academic discussions like this chapter), because characters act, and acts reveal character.

The art of characterization in ancient texts is terse while in modern texts it tends to be fulsome. Thus, we must use a different set of conventions to read the old texts well. The two primary vehicles Old Testament narrators use to depict character are words and deeds; that is, through what characters say and do narrators convey personality, attributes, and motivation. Nearly 50 percent of Hebrew narrative is dialogue, but characters' quoted words are compressed so that every word tells. As Bar-Efrat explains, "Conversations in biblical narrative are never precise and naturalistic imitations of real-life conversations. They are highly concentrated and stylized, are devoid of idle chatter, and all the details they contain are carefully calculated to fulfill a clear function."[15] When Adam blames his wife and, by implication, God, the storyteller reveals the first man's spiritual state. Adam attempts to cover his own sin by deflecting responsibility. Through dialogue, the narrator reveals character.

Action also conveys character. Old Testament scholar Richard Pratt demonstrates this in the story of Ehud (Judg. 3:12–30).[16] Ehud is a man of skill, which we know because he makes his own double-edged sword. He possesses physical strength as seen when he thrusts the sword all the way into Eglon's body. We know that he is trustworthy because the people entrust their tribute to him. We know that he is brave because he faces Eglon alone, and he is crafty in his strategy and escape. Eglon, the antagonist, is a pitiless despot who oppresses the Israelites. He is also a fool because he leaves himself unguarded. The use of action to depict character is subtle, but this is the craft of Old Testament narrative. The authors show more than they tell.

Other techniques of Old Testament characterization are:

Titles and names. Rahab is a "prostitute" (Josh. 2:1), Elisha is the "man of God" (2 Kings 5:8), and Naaman is the "commander of the army of the king of Aram" (2 Kings 5:1). "Abram" ("father") becomes "Abraham" ("Father of many nations"). In his old age he bears "Laughter," who in turn bears a boy named "Deceiver" and then "Prince of God." The closer kinsman who accedes to Boaz does not even have a name. He is *peloni almoni*, a vague Hebrew phrase meaning "Mr. So-and-so." Thus is this shirker memorialized for all generations. He tried to preserve his name by refusing poor Ruth, but he ended up with no name. When reading Hebrew narratives, we modern, western readers need to use the same set of expectations we bring to Dickens, who creates characters like "Uriah Heep" and "Ebenezer Scrooge." Names communicate character. Authors use names to point the arrows of audience expectation.

Physical description. Biblical narrators are notably laconic in this matter. They rarely describe the outer person, so that when they do tell us that Sarah was beautiful, Esau was hairy, or that Ehud was left-handed, they want us to perceive character that will impact plot. For example, the author of 2 Samuel suggests Absalom's handsome virility by describing his long hair that weighed 200 shekels (2 Sam. 14:26). In Hebrew culture, long hair was associated with strength. The description helps explain how Absalom stole the people's hearts and foreshadows the irony of being caught and killed by that hair. Another physical description, that of Goliath, may be the most fulsome in the entire Bible (1 Sam. 17:4–7), but even that depiction takes only three verses. Hebrew storytellers paint with the quick strokes of watercolor, not the painstaking brushing of oil. As stated above, the author depicts the Philistine warrior as a technological and biological terror. His defeat at the hands of a boy is surely the work of God.

Foils. A "foil" is a deliberate contrast to the protagonist. When Orpah returns to Moab, we see Ruth's loyalty and courage in a stronger light. When Lot chooses the well-watered plains of Sodom, we admire Abraham's discernment.

Much more could be said about Hebrew techniques of characterization, but this is enough to demonstrate that those authors employed a subtle and artistic craft. But to what end? How does characterization function rhetorically to advance the author's intention? It does so by prompting identification. As Pratt states, "Old Testament authors did not present characters simply to tell their readers about people in the past but to evoke responses. . . . Old Testament writers intended for many of their characters to elicit sympathetic responses of approval. Characters take on the qualities of heroes or models of appropriate attitudes and behavior that the audience was expected to appreciate and admire."[17] When our minds are caught up in the action and our hearts are bound to the characters, story works its magic. When a narrator begins with "Once upon a time," listeners relax, drop their guard, and yield to the form of the genre. Then the ideas associated with that form find unencumbered access to the heart. Conversely, defense mechanisms snap to attention when we suspect an argument, for we know the speaker is trying to change us, and none of us likes that!

The rhetorical function of identification is easily transported to the sermon if we use imagination to help the listeners empathize with the characters. When told vividly, listeners can flee vicariously with Joseph from Potiphar's wife and perhaps flee twenty-first-century temptation as well. Expositors can help listeners identify with biblical characters by describing the culture and circumstances of the ancient world, or by using current examples, self-disclosure, and testimony. However it is done, we can serve our listeners by using the inductive, subtle, beguiling techniques of story whereby we show the truth, not simply assert it. Disciples learn by example and are inspired by models.

Setting

The final element that makes a story a story is "setting"—the time and place where the characters act. As with physical descriptions of characters, Old Testament narrators are extremely selective with details of setting, yet every word counts. On the surface, all we seem to know about the setting of Ruth is that the story takes place "in the days when the judges ruled" (1:1), opens in Bethlehem, shifts to Moab, and then shifts back to Bethlehem. This paucity of description can bore modern readers, who are fascinated by the innards of submarines described in *The Hunt for Red October* by Tom Clancy and the quiet of southern courtrooms described in *The Runaway Jury* by John Grisham, so modern readers must learn to read again.

Look again at Ruth. The story bristles with setting. Perhaps the author calls attention to "the days when the judges ruled" to create a foil. This gem of a story shines more brightly because the author sets it in the midst of Israel's dark ages. The author communicates mood and theology with the quick strokes of watercolor. With efficient brushwork describing Elimelech's move from Bethlehem to Moab, the author implies disloyalty to the covenant and lack of faith. Thus, setting contributes to plot and character. Indeed, the three aspects of narrative—plot, character, and setting—form a unified medium of communication.

Notice some other strokes of setting in Ruth: the reader imaginatively enters "a field belonging to Boaz" (2:3), takes a "short rest in the shelter" (2:7), and is transported to town (2:18), the threshing floor (3:6), and the town gate (4:1). The clock spins as Ruth gleans "until evening" (2:17), and Boaz discovers Ruth "in the middle of the night" (3:8). The calendar rustles through the barley and wheat harvests (1:22; 2:23). Setting abounds in this story for those who have eyes to see. If the author tells us that a scene takes place in fields of ripe grain, or in Moab, or in the city gates, enquiring minds take note.

Depiction of setting serves two rhetorical functions. The first is the sparking of imagination. Readers of Old Testament narrative hear the sounds of wind in the desert, smell the aromas of the temple, and feel the lurch of the waves shove the tiny ships of that day. Using tools such as atlases, encyclopedias, handbooks, and commentaries, exegetes discover details of setting that make the story come alive, and then as preachers, those exegetes use vivid language to transport hearers to the ancient time and place. Here is an example from Eugene Peterson who describes David in the caves of En-Gedi:

> David and a few of his men are hidden in a cave in the cliffs above the Dead Sea. The day is hot and the cave is cool. They're deep in the cave, resting. Suddenly there's a shadow across the mouth of the cave; they're astonished to see that it's King Saul. . . . Saul enters the cave but doesn't see them: fresh from the hard glare of the desert sun, his eyes aren't adjusted to the darkness.[18]

When sparking imagination, an objection arises: imagination can lead to inaccuracy. After all, the text does not say that the day was hot. That day might have seen a rare rain shower. My response to this legitimate objection is twofold. First, careful exegesis supplies all the food for imagination preachers need. Use your study tools to lead out all that the storyteller put in. The original author knew where En-Gedi was and what kind of terrain it encompasses, and he presumably intended that we supply that same knowledge when reading the account. If this was not his intention, he would not have mentioned the setting, but since modern readers are separated from the story by thousands of years and thousands of miles, we must hit the books. When we do so, we enable ourselves to lead out what the author has put in without going beyond what he has put in. Careful study sparks the imagination.

Second, when in doubt about the exact details of setting (such as the heat of the day), qualify your statements with phrases like, "It was probably hot, blistering hot, since the average temperature in that part of the world is. . . ." Brief qualifications like this do not undermine the rhetorical impact of imagination, but they might preserve us from "flights of fancy."

In addition to imagination, a second rhetorical function is association. Scholars such as Northrop Frye and John Sailhamer demonstrate convincingly that the Bible is *one* book.[19] Although written by scores of people over thousands of years, it remains a cohesive, self-reflective constellation of meaning. Parts allude to other parts, and authors count on readers to catch the allusions, understanding individual narratives in light of the metanarrative of redemptive history. Thus, the author of Ruth intends the reader to hear the sweet music of this story of redemption against the cacophonous jangle of anarchy in "the days of the judges." The author expects the reader to possess prior knowledge about the Land and the Deuteronomic covenant so that a brief mention of migrating from Bethlehem to Moab points the arrows of our expectation toward tragedy. Through associations, the narrators communicate theology, but once again, their craft is subtle. They embody ideas in persons and places.

Biblical preachers can unleash the rhetoric of association in two ways. First, we can simply explain the allusions. We preachers are, in part, teachers, and we need not hesitate to unpack what God has packed in. Of course, good teachers do not simply regurgitate information. They engage the listeners with the relevance of the material. Second, in our sermons from Old Testament narratives, we should return again and again to the metanarrative. Over time, as we interpret these stories on the "top level," our listeners will come to possess their own body of prior knowledge so that they make associations themselves. They will see the Old Testament as the grand story of creation, rebellion, and redemption. They will place themselves, as the authors intended, in the majestic flow of God's story.

Conclusion

Plot, character, and setting are the frequencies the Hebrew storytellers used to transmit truth. Only by attuning our ears to those frequencies can we hear the truth as the authors intended it to be heard, as narrative rhetoric that captures attention, prompts identification, and sparks imagination. After listening well, we preachers are well-equipped to rebroadcast the message to contemporary listeners through the enchanting medium of story.

Questions to Consider

1. What are the five stages involved in plot structure?
2. How is character depicted in Old Testament narratives?
3. What is the function of setting in narratives?
4. Reflect on how you can take the tips from this chapter and put them into practice in your sermon preparation. What's your plan?

On the Shelf

Alter, Robert. *The Art of Biblical Narrative.* New York: Basic, 1981.

Larsen, David. *Telling the Old, Old Story: The Art of Narrative Preaching.* Grand Rapids: Kregel, 1995.

Lowry, Eugene L. *The Homiletical Plot: The Sermon as Narrative Art Form.* Expanded edition. Louisville: Westminster John Knox, 2000.

Mathewson, Steven D. *The Art of Preaching Old Testament Narrative.* Grand Rapids: Baker, 2002.

Pratt, Richard L. *He Gave Us Stories: The Bible Student's Guide to Interpreting Old Testament Narratives.* Brentwood, TN: Wolgemuth & Hyatt, 1990.

5

Preaching from the Law

Douglas K. Stuart

My remarks in this chapter[1] indeed relate to *preparing* to preach, rather than preaching itself. That is, they are not in the form of an instruction manual with examples, but in the form of an evaluation of the viewpoint from which we preach the Old Testament law—the foundational considerations that call us to the task and orient our commitment rather than a discussion of techniques for delivery of Old Testament sermons.

It is a joy to dedicate these words to Walter Kaiser. If anyone is a model of faithfully preaching the whole counsel of God, he is. He loves God's law—just as it was intended to be loved eventually by new covenant believers when first revealed to old covenant believers in the days of Moses. Kaiser well understands what many people often fail to realize: that God knew perfectly well that there would be a twenty-first century AD back when he was inspiring Moses to write down the Old Testament law, and that the words God revealed in that law would remain essential information—in fact, life-and-death stuff—for believers of all ages, not just Old Testament Israelites.

Why We Avoid Preaching the Law

Yet we avoid preaching the law because we're scared that it won't seem relevant. Everybody wants relevance. Most people instinctively, though erroneously, define relevance as "advice I can use this week to make my life happier." This puts a message-distorting pressure on those of us who preach because the easiest and fastest way to please people who think of relevance that way is to give them warm, friendly, human wisdom that they will readily perceive as practical and immediately useful. In such an enterprise, most parts of the Bible, and certainly the Old Testament law, may seem to offer little or no help. And woe to the preacher who comes across as not helpful! If people think that your sermons don't help them, they'll certainly figure out some way to show it, via reduced attendance at worship, or a remarkably consistent disinterest in increasing your salary, or even a desire to move you on to some other church where they assume you can bore some other group of people. That's scary!

Why We Shouldn't Avoid Preaching the Law

Scary or not, we need the law. That's because our main challenges are moral. There's something to be said for the challenges of technological progress, but such progress can't save anyone from sin or, in fact, do much more for a person who resists the gospel than to make that person's trip toward hell more comfortable. There's much to be said for education, but academic skill of all sorts is ultimately mainly human wisdom, and well-educated people seem to have plenty of ability to be miserable, or impractical, or both. There's a lot to be said for world cooperation, that is, political, social, and economic cooperation among nations, but its best results are merely temporal, and its results so far throughout history have not been notably impressive. (Can anyone prove that the world is a better place now than it was a hundred years ago?) Any human endeavor that seeks to make people's lives happier is worthy, but a happy life on this planet is a thing far short of God's goal for us: eternal life with him where he lives, amid joys so wonderful they are impossible to describe in the present. And what keeps us from that? Immorality, also known as sin.

So how are we to understand the nature of sin and therefore be able to seek God's help in avoiding it as we try to live as his covenant people? The answer is that we need to understand what he likes and dislikes. Much of this he has stated *only* in the Old Testament, assuming that we would not need to have it restated verbatim in the New.[2]

How can the employee please the boss if the employee does not take the trouble to learn what the boss wants done and what the boss has prohibited? In the new covenant, believers please God by following Christ with the help of God's Spirit, who prompts and prods thinking and action that would otherwise be merely human with all its sinful limitations. Can the Holy Spirit use our knowledge of the Old Testament law to inform our perspectives and give us not only examples but a general framework for sensing what sort of thinking and behavior would please God under the new covenant? Of course he can—and indeed, that is just how he, the author of the old covenant law, expects us to view the material that he authored via his prophet Moses.

That is, then, what the Old Testament law does for us as the Spirit uses it. Those who follow Christ must recognize that the Pentateuchal law is not *our covenant* law (that is, most of it has not been brought over into the new covenant from the old and therefore its commands that were direct commands to the Israelites are not direct commands to us). But this does not mean that the law somehow ceases to be the *Word of God* for us. On the analogy of the way that Old Testament narratives or Old Testament wisdom teachings *guide* us even though they don't necessarily contain direct *commands* to us, the law continues to have direct relevance and usefulness even though we are under a newer covenant.

Especially important is the fact that the law is a place where we can find out the kinds of standards that the same God who currently expects us to know him and obey him originally placed before his chosen people so that they might know him and obey him. In other words, the principles of the law have not become irrelevant to the life of the believer just because of the passage of time. What the law continues to do for us is to give us principles about what God expects in human behavior, principles that are hugely helpful in guiding us as we respond to the Holy Spirit's leading to follow Christ.

How It Should Be Done in Principle

In any preaching from the law it is important to get across early and often the following simple but crucial concept: *No rules, no relationship*. That's the essence of what people need to understand about the value of the law for them as they seek to follow Christ. The law wasn't—and isn't—there to make us busy keeping rules so we won't get into trouble; it's there because through it God's people were brought into relationship with him. Biblical laws are *covenant* stipulations: a means of formally connecting two parties (God and his people) with all the benefits that the connection provides.

We live in an age and a culture in which it is assumed that no-fault, no-pressure, no-rules relationships are not only possible (they aren't) but desirable (again, they aren't). For example, many couples try a form of imitation "marriage" in which they simply move in together, stay together as long as it suits both of them, and then split when one or both find it convenient to do so. This sort of arrangement is easy, but it isn't much of a relationship. The children of such relationships are at the mercy of the moment for any stability of connection with their parents; the benefits of long-term family interaction are virtually unknown; the likelihood of loneliness in middle- and old-age is high; and so on. In other words, in a no-rules relationship, the benefits are small, and the miseries potentially far greater.

But in a rules relationship (a covenant), lasting benefits are the goal—the purpose for the rules. If the rules are known and kept, blessings come in abundance. The one who gives the covenant to his people gives it precisely out of a desire for their benefit, that they might enjoy him and his goodness forever.

The Old Testament covenant, the law, occurs formally in Exodus, Leviticus, Numbers, and Deuteronomy. Exodus-Leviticus forms a covenant that is supplemented by the laws revealed over time in Numbers, somewhat in the way that the Constitution of the United States has been supplemented by its amendments over time. Deuteronomy, on the other hand, is a self-contained covenant, a restatement and reorganization of the original Exodus-Leviticus-Numbers covenant for the second and subsequent generations of Israelites.

For our illustrative purposes in this chapter, we can focus on the Exodus-Leviticus covenant. We should note that the strictly covenant portion of the book of Exodus (20:1–31:18) finds completion only in the book of Leviticus as indicated by the closing words of Leviticus, "These are the commands the Lord gave Moses on Mount Sinai for the Israelites" (Lev. 27:34). In other words, Exodus gets the Sinai covenant underway, but does not complete it.

It is important to note that the structure of the legal portion of Exodus is patterned after those of ancient covenants known as "suzerainty treaties," where a conqueror made a treaty with the conquered in which he "benefited" them with his protection and care as long as they would abide by the treaty stipulations.[3] There are normally six parts to such covenants, summarized here with the coordinates that relate the structure to Exodus:

1. Prologue: which identifies the giver of the covenant ("the Lord your God," 20:2)
2. Preamble: a reminder of the relationship of the suzerain to the people ("who brought you out of Egypt," 20:2)
3. Stipulations: various laws/obligations on the part of the people (20:3–23:19; 25:1–31:18)
4. List of witnesses to the covenant ("I am the Lord [Yahweh] their God," Exod. 29:46; 31:13; Lev. 11:44)[4]

5. Document clause: providing for writing down of the covenant so that periodic reading and relearning of the covenant can take place as time goes by (see Exod. 24:4, 7, 12)
6. Sanctions: blessings and curses as incentives for obedience (see Exod. 20:5–6, 12, 24; 23:20–31; cf. Lev. 26:3–14 [blessings]; 26:14–39 [curses]; 26:40–45 [restoration blessings])

Only four of the six covenant ingredients are found in Exodus, mainly in the so-called covenant code (20:1–23:32). This is because Exodus is only the first portion of the full covenant that continues on in Leviticus and receives supplemental stipulations in Numbers.[5] Moreover, the Sinai covenant is only the first statement of the full Pentateuchal or Mosaic covenant, which finally concludes at the end of Deuteronomy. Nevertheless, already in Exodus the essential elements of the covenant are obvious: the revelation of who God is and what he wants of his people,[6] and obedience to God as the path of covenant loyalty and thus of its blessings.[7]

Within this overall framework, let us take some key rules as paradigmatic for the way that rules provide the structure for the relationship that the covenant is given to establish. It should be noted at the outset that nothing in Exodus 20, where the so-called Ten Commandments are found, is described as "commandment" or "law" or the like.[8] To be sure, the words presented here by God do indeed command his people most solemnly to act in ways that are basic to his covenant, but their significance goes beyond that of routine "laws." What Exodus 20 contains—in particular, the Ten "Words" (*hadevarim*)—is more like the content of a national constitution than merely like the content of one section of codified law or another. If the American legal corpus is used as an analogy, it could be said that the ten "words" of Exodus 20 are somewhat like the Constitution of the United States (legally binding in a most basic, foundational way, but more than a mere set of individual laws) and the laws that follow (cf. 21:1, "These are the laws that you are to set before them. . . .") are somewhat analogous to the various sections of federal law dealing with all sorts of particular matters that have been enacted legislatively over time. The one group is absolutely "constitutional" or "foundational"; the other is specifically regulatory, following from the principles articulated in the more basic "constitution." It is both traditional and convenient to call them "the Ten Commandments," as long as their special nature is recognized. Indeed, in the comment that Moses speaks following the repeat of the Ten Commandments in Deuteronomy 5:6–21, he explicitly calls them "commandments" ("These are the commandments the Lord proclaimed in a loud voice to your whole assembly there on the mountain. . . ." Deut. 5:22).

The biblical commandments occur in three levels of specificity. At the most comprehensive level are the "two great commandments" of Deuteronomy 6:5 ("Love the Lord your God with all your heart and with all your soul and with all your strength") and Leviticus 19:18b ("love your neighbor as yourself"). The first of these requires in broad terms a loyal, covenantal obedience to God, who is put first above all other relationships.[9] The second requires loving (loyal) treatment of other human beings. Jesus gave his approval to what had become in Judaism an understanding of the importance of the two great commandments as summations of all the others.[10] He also specifically indicated that the rest of the commandments "hang on" these two (Matt. 22:40). How so? The first four of the Ten Commandments hang on the command to love God, since they describe ways to show covenant loyalty directly to him. The final six hang on the command to love neighbor as self, which Jesus also explained as doing to others as you would have them do to you (Matt. 7:12). Thus, the first four "vertical" commandments are balanced by the final six "horizontal" commandments which represent a second level. Then, in order of hierarchy, follow all the others as a third level. Thus the order is the two, the ten, and the 601.[11] Some of the large group of 601 remaining commandments address "vertical" concerns; others speak of the "horizontal."

How, then, can these ten "words"—or even the remaining 601 commandments—provide adequate coverage for all the myriad human challenges and experiences, temptations and sins that one encounters or commits in a lifetime? How can so few laws serve to guide so many people in so many cultures in so complex a life as we live on this planet?

The answer is that biblical law is *paradigmatic,* and that from it principles for living in obedience to God are to be derived. It is these principles that the preacher must identify and bring to the attention of others, always using the New Testament as a guide for identifying how the various parts of the law have relevance for New Testament believers.

Modern societies, by contrast, have generally opted for exhaustive law codes. That is, every action that the modern society wishes to regulate or prohibit must be specifically mentioned in a separate law. Under the expectations of this exhaustive law system, state or federal law codes run to thousands of pages and address thousands of individual actions by way of requirement or restriction or control or banning of those actions. By this approach, all actions are permitted that are not expressly forbidden or regulated. Thus it is not uncommon that criminals evade prosecution because of a "technicality" or a "loophole" in the law—their undesirable actions are not *exactly* prohibited or regulated by a written law, so they cannot be convicted even though an objective observer is convinced that what they did surely deserved punishment.

Ancient laws did not work this way. They were paradigmatic, giving models of behaviors and models of prohibitions/punishments relative to those behaviors, but they made no attempt to be exhaustive. An example of this phenomenon of paradigmatic law is found in the way that the individual statutes of the famous Law of Hammurabi (from about 1720 BC) were never cited in the ancient world as determinative for actual court cases, even though they were, in fact, determinative for those court cases. Thousands of court records from the ancient Mesopotamian world of Hammurabi's time and the decades and centuries thereafter have been uncovered, well-preserved because they are written in cuneiform on clay tablets that have survived the ages. None of these court records ever refers to Hammurabi's Law, in spite of their careful detail in recording cases that are of the exact sort that Hammurabi's Law gives guidance to judges on how to rule in such cases. Why is this so? Because everyone in the ancient world understood that law codes were paradigms to be extrapolated from, not exhaustive lists of penalties or actions to be taken in a given sort of legal situation. In other words, judges in a court case looked to law codes for *examples of the sort of justice that should prevail.* They still made their own decisions and gave forth their own rulings—using law codes as *models*, not as specific prescriptions, of how to rule judiciously.[12]

Ancient laws gave guiding principles, or samples, rather than complete descriptions of all things regulated. That's what the preacher must get across when preaching Old Testament law to a modern audience. Ancient people were expected to be able to extrapolate from what the sampling of laws did say to the *general* behavior that the laws in their totality pointed toward. That's our task, too. Ancient judges were expected to extrapolate from the wording provided in the laws that did exist to *all other* circumstances, and not to be foiled in their jurisprudence by any such concepts as "technicalities" or "loopholes." When common sense told judges[13] that a crime had been committed, they reasoned their way from whatever the most nearly applicable law required to a decision as to how to administer proper justice in the case before them. Citizens of ancient Israel, and especially its judges, had to learn to extrapolate from whatever laws they had received from Yahweh to whatever justice-challenging situation they were dealing with. The number of laws dealing with any given application of justice might be few, but that would not prevent justice from being applied. It would simply have been the case that all parties were expected to appeal for guidance to those laws that did exist, whether expressed specifically in terms that dealt with the case under consideration or not. In other words, the Israelites had to learn to see the underlying principles in any law and not let the specifics of the individual casuistic citation mislead them into applying the law too narrowly. We face the same sort of expectation in our use of Old Testament law.

God's revealed covenant law to Israel was paradigmatic. No Israelite could say, "The law says I must make restitution for stolen oxen or sheep (Exod. 22:1) but I stole your goat; I don't have to pay you back," or "The law says that anyone who attacks his father or mother must be put to death (Exod. 21:15) but I attacked my grandmother, so I shouldn't be punished," or "The law says that certain penalties apply for hitting someone with a fist or a stone (Exod. 21:18), but I kicked my neighbor with my foot and hit him with a piece of wood, so I shouldn't be punished." Such arguments would have insulted the intelligence of all concerned and made no impact on those rendering judgments. It is in connection with the paradigmatic nature of Israel's covenant law that Jesus, following the established tradition in Judaism, can make so sweeping an assertion as that two laws sum up all the rest (see above).

Properly understood, two laws do indeed sum up *everything* in the entire legal corpus of the Old Testament. So do ten laws (the Ten Words/Commandments); so do all 613. The numbers go no higher, nor would they need to. If a reasonable number of comprehensive and comprehensible laws (as few as 2, as many as 613) are promulgated to a people as paradigms for proper living, there is no excuse for people to claim ignorance of how to behave or innocence when their sins are found out. Most laws are expressed as commands in the masculine singular—the *you* of the laws is "you, a male person," from a technical, grammatical point of view, but the reader/listener would have not the slightest ground to say, "It prohibits individual men from doing such and such, but I'm a woman/we're a group, so the wording of the law exempts me/us." Implicit in the wording is the need for paradigmatic extrapolation to all persons, singular or plural, male or female. That's what the modern preacher does, too—as and only as the New Testament shows the way.

Within the new covenant, the paradigm of the two great laws is summarized as the "law of Christ" (Gal. 6:2). Because of the help of the Holy Spirit, the need to memorize and remember hundreds of commandments is obviated. The law is no longer a matter of (paradigmatic) guidelines written externally on tablets of stone; it is now a matter of a clear sense of loving God and neighbor written on the heart by God's Spirit (Jer. 31:31–34;

cf. Rom. 2:15) in accordance with the two commandments that always summed up God's will, or the ten that in the old covenant were necessary to clarify the two and all the rest that clarify the particulars.

One may ask, "If the commands to love God with one's whole heart and to love neighbor as self are the two greatest, why weren't these the first commandments spoken at Sinai? Why did one of them ('love your neighbor as yourself,' Lev. 19:18b) come later to the attention of the Israelites rather subtly, without fanfare, in the midst of the levitical 'Holiness Code' (Leviticus 19–26) and the other ('love God with all your heart,' Deut. 6:5) almost forty years later, in the new generation's law code, Deuteronomy"? The answer is disarmingly simple: too many people could not appreciate the two great commandments except in reference to the others, including the ten principal expressions thereof, the Ten Words/Commandments of Exodus 20.

That is, without an awareness of all 613 commandments and seeing within them the high standards of God's holiness and his particular required or banned behaviors enumerated, a person corrupted by a fallen world does not easily get the point of what it is that the two great commandments are intended to summarize. Once one has learned the breadth and depth of God's expectations for his holy people, however, the two greatest commandments serve brilliantly as comprehensive reminders of all that is expected of God's covenant people. This is the point of the law of Christ in the new covenant: It is not an amorphous, contentless concept, but a way of summarizing full obedience to everything Christ taught, demonstrated, and reinforced elsewhere in Scripture, built upon the specifics of the Old Testament law.

A final implication of paradigmatic law: Not all laws will be equally comprehensive in scope. That is, some will be very broad in their applicability (love Yahweh your God) and some much more narrow (do not bear false witness). One might ask, "Why not say, 'don't be dishonest in any way,' which would be broader and more comprehensive than 'don't bear false witness'"? But that would be missing the way that paradigmatic law works: The reader or listener comes to understand that all sorts of situations not exactly specified (because a law is either so broad or so narrow) are also implicitly covered by a somewhat randomly presented admixture of rather specific examples of more general behaviors and very general regulations of broad categories of behavior. In other words, when all the laws are considered together, one's impression is that both the very narrow, precise issues and the very broad, general issues fall under the purview of God's covenant. The wide variability of comprehensiveness is supposed to help the person desiring to keep the covenant to say, "I now see that in the tiniest detail as well as in the widest, most general way, I am expected to try to keep this law—in all its implications, not just in terms of its exact wording." Some commandments are thus less broad in scope *in the way they are expressed* than is necessary to cover all the intended actions; others are so broad in scope *in the way they are expressed* that one could never think up all the ways they might be applied. This is just as it should be. The narrow and the broad taken together suggest the overall comprehensiveness of God's covenant will for his people.[14]

Jesus was a lawgiver. He expected obedience to his commands, as the Great Commission says:

> Go therefore and make disciples of all nations, baptizing them in the name of the Father and of the Son and of the Holy Spirit, and teaching them to *obey everything that I have commanded you*. And remember that I am with you always, to the end of the age.
>
> Matthew 28:19 NRSV, emphasis added

Did he make up all those commands afresh? Did he intend that the commands from the Old Testament law were to be ignored? Hardly. He stated his desire relative to the law very clearly:

> Think not that I have come to abolish the law and the prophets; I have come not to abolish them but to fulfil them. For truly, I say to you, till heaven and earth pass away, not an iota, not a dot, will pass from the law until all is accomplished. Whoever

> then relaxes one of the least of these commandments and teaches men so, shall be called least in the kingdom of heaven; but he who does them and teaches them shall be called great in the kingdom of heaven. For I tell you, unless your righteousness exceeds that of the scribes and Pharisees, you will never enter the kingdom of heaven.
>
> Matthew 5:17–20 RSV

We suggest that by these words Jesus both required and empowered us to preach the law—not as our *covenant*, because he made a new one in his blood that supercedes the old (Luke 22:20; 1 Cor. 11:25), but as principles derived from paradigms to guide us into holy living under his new covenant: an obligation for every disciple, and therefore a preaching responsibility for every expositor of the Word.

Questions to Consider

1. How does the Holy Spirit use Old Testament law in the lives of Christians today?
2. What is the essence that people need to understand about the value of the law for them today?
3. What does the author mean when he says biblical law is paradigmatic?
4. How is the law of Christ built on Old Testament law and how are we to preach it?

On the Shelf

(Note: The following books are mainly about biblical law from a nonevangelical perspective, but contain information that an interested evangelical can benefit from.)

Boecker, Hans Jochen. *Law and the Administration of Justice in the Old Testament and the Ancient Near East.* Minneapolis: Augsburg, 1980.

Carmichael, Calum. *The Spirit of Biblical Law.* Athens, GA: University of Georgia Press, 1996.

Daube, David. *Studies in Biblical Law.* Cambridge: Cambridge University Press, 1947. Reprint, London: Lawbook Exchange, 2004.

Doorly, William J. *The Laws of Yahweh: A Handbook of Biblical Law.* Mahwah, NJ: Paulist Press, 2002.

Phillips, Anthony. *Essays on Biblical Law.* Sheffield, UK: Sheffield Academic Press, 2003.

6

Preaching from the Psalms and Proverbs

Duane A. Garrett

The Importance of Structure

Walter C. Kaiser Jr. has two fundamental rules for preaching that he hammers home to his audiences at every opportunity. The first is, "Keep your finger on the text!" (in other words, proclaim what the biblical passage actually says and let it be your authority). The other rule, not always directly stated but always modeled, is that the structure of the passage should determine the structure or content of the message. At preaching opportunities, Kaiser frequently makes the structural analysis of the text he is preaching available to his congregation. He wants them to see how he came to the conclusions he has reached, and he also wants to give them an example of how to turn the structure of a biblical passage into a contemporary sermon.

In few places is this method more applicable than in the proclamation of texts from Psalms and Proverbs. Every psalm is of course a discrete poem, and thus every psalm can be analyzed to determine its structure. With the structure established, the preacher can use it to guide him in understanding the major divisions of the psalm, and from that have a better understanding of its central message and of the main points it makes. In most cases, the psalmist's meaning and message will in some way be reflected in the structure of the psalm, and often understanding a psalm's structure can significantly clarify what it's all about.

Of course, some psalms are so lengthy that preaching a single sermon that covers the whole psalm may be impractical. Even in these cases, however, knowing the structure of the whole will help the preacher deliver a sermon that accurately reflects the message of the psalm. Also, in these cases, the preacher should select a portion of the text that has structural integrity; in other words, he will want to select a passage that is a discrete section of the psalm rather than selecting a group of verses that straddle two different sections. For example, the obvious structure of Psalm 119 is that it is an acrostic of twenty-two sections built upon the letters of the Hebrew alphabet. A pastor could give a sermon that reflects the meaning of the entire psalm but do a close exposition of only one of the twenty-two sections (one could focus, for example, on the *beth* section in verses 9–16).

In suggesting that analyzing the structure of the text is a critical step in the preparation of a sermon, I am not suggesting either that analyzing the structure is simple or that it is a simple matter to know what to do with the structure after one has found it. For the most part, the structure of a biblical poem will follow familiar patterns. Sometimes the structure will be simple parallelism (the poem will have a basic structure of A–B–C–A′–B′–C′, or something similar) or chiasmus (like A–B–C–C′–B′–A′). Sometimes the structure may involve the repetition of a key word or line (for example, a particular word may appear at the beginning of each stanza). A refrain may separate major stanzas. Sometimes it is more subtle; for example, a change in metaphor may signal a new stanza.

Interpreters should generally be wary of hierarchical outlines unless there are clear markers in the Hebrew text. Such outlines are modern, western devices and they are notoriously arbitrary as applied to Hebrew poetry. That is, each interpreter will often see whatever outline he wants to see, and there are few controls for evaluating the superiority of one outline over another. It is, of course, much better to look for structure in a Hebrew psalm instead of in an English translation. Finally, there is no guarantee that the structure we think we see in a text is actually there. Like everything else in literary interpretation, a structural analysis of a Hebrew poem is to a degree subjective, depends upon the skill of the interpreter, and will be only as certain as it is clear and straightforward in the text. A poem with a complex or subtle structure will be difficult to analyze.

But what does one do with a psalm after one has determined the probable structure of the text? One can make the structure of the psalm the actual outline of the sermon. That is, if a psalm has four major stanzas, each one making a major point, then one could preach a four-point sermon that strictly follows the structure and text of the psalm. This sometimes works well but, in my view, often it does not. For various reasons, using the structure of the psalm as the outline of the sermon may be impossible. First, a psalm is a poem (or song), and its structure is in part determined by the need for it to succeed as a poem. What works well in a poem may not work well in a speech. Second, there may be repetition in a psalm, where one stanza in large measure repeats an earlier stanza. In a sermon, obviously, one does not want two major points that say the same thing. Third, and most commonly, the psalm may have a structure that is simply too long or complex to work well as a sermon.

For example, Psalm 112 is another simple acrostic; in this case, it is twenty-two lines long, with each succeeding line beginning with a successive letter of the Hebrew alphabet. In my view, that is essentially all there is to say about the structure of the psalm: it is twenty-two individual lines, with each one making a point about the life and qualities of the righteous man over against those of the wicked man. One can try to group these lines into larger stanzas, but such stanzas are arbitrarily created by the interpreter and in reality undermine the simplicity of the psalm itself, which gives us in alphabetical order twenty-two one-line declarations about the righteous man. Plainly, no one wants to hear a twenty-two-point sermon (and such a sermon would involve repetition of the unhelpful kind described above; compare verse 3b, "and his righteousness endures forever," to verse 9b). It would be better to preach a sermon that, like the psalm, describes the life and qualities of the righteous, but do it without slavishly following the order of the psalm. Thus, by citing verses 4b, 5a, and 9a, one could include in the sermon the point that the righteous are characterized by generosity and compassion. Such a message would be true to both the structure and content of the psalm without falling into the trap of preaching a sermon that is no more than a running homily on the text.

Preaching Proverbs

In preaching from Proverbs, one immediately confronts the fact that there are two basic text types. First, there are wisdom poems, which make up Proverbs 1–9 and 31:10–31 (and arguably 31:1–9). These poems are similar to psalms but generally have a fairly straightforward structure (psalms are often more complex). As such, they can be analyzed for structure and made into sermons in a rather direct fashion, although, as is the case with psalms, the outline of the wisdom poem may not transfer directly into a sermon. Second, there are the collections of individual aphorisms or proverbs that make up Proverbs 10–30. Preaching from these chapters is much more of a challenge, but the same principles outlined above still apply.

Wisdom Poems

The structure of the wisdom poem of Proverbs 2 leads fairly directly into its interpretation and thus into what kind of message one could preach using this text. Its structure is as follows:

1. Threefold protasis (vv. 1–4)
   a. If (Hebrew: *im*) you accept wisdom (vv. 1–2)
   b. If (*im*) you call out for understanding (v. 3)
   c. If (*im*) you search for wisdom like treasure (v. 4)
2. Complex apodosis (vv. 5–22)
   a. Initial results (vv. 5–11)
      i. Then (Hebrew: *az*) you will understand the fear of the Lord (vv. 5–8)
      ii. Then (*az*) you will understand what is right (vv. 9–11)
   b. Secondary results (vv. 12–19)
      i. This will keep you (Hebrew: *lehatstsilka*) from criminal associations (vv. 12–15)
      ii. This will keep you (*lehatstsilka*) from promiscuous women (vv. 16–19)
   c. Final outcome (vv. 20–22): Things will turn out so that (Hebrew: *lema'an*) your whole life will be upright instead of corrupt

The first major division, verses 1–4, is made up of three smaller strophes, each of which begins with *im* ("if"), establishing the entire poem as a giant conditional statement ("if you do X, then Y will follow"). Everything that follows, verses 5–22, is the outcome or apodosis that comes from fulfilling the "if" clause. As indicated above, it is in three parts. The first two sections (vv. 5–8, 9–11) each begin with the Hebrew word *az* ("then") and serve to give the immediate results: the reader, here called "my son," will gain the fear of the Lord and an understanding of right and wrong. The next two sections (vv. 12–15, 16–19) both begin with the Hebrew *lehatstsilka* (literally, "to keep you") and give the secondary outcome: the reader will associate neither with violent men nor with prostitutes. The last section (vv. 20–22) begins with *lema'an* ("so that, with the result that") and gives a kind of summation or final outcome: the reader's entire life will be governed by right principles and he will be included among the righteous. Throughout the poem there are many explanatory lines that further illuminate or explain what the text is saying. These sometimes begin with

Hebrew *ki* ("because"), but they do not mark new divisions in the poem; they are simply additional exhortation and clarification within the larger structure described above. Thus, for example, in the section on the immoral woman (vv. 16–19), the reader is told that avoiding such a woman is wise and good "because (*ki*) her house descends to death" (v. 18a).

In order to understand fully and to proclaim Proverbs 2, it is essential that one appreciate a basic fact about the intended audience of this and of all of Proverbs: it is addressed to the young man, here called "my son." That is, the text primarily exhorts young men whose path in life is not yet set; they are old enough to begin to feel the attractions of crime and sex, but not so old that their life's path is already set. They are, in short, adolescent males. Awareness of this enables us to understand why so much of Proverbs 1–10 is taken up with violence, crime, and the promise of easy money, on the one hand, and with immoral women, on the other hand. These are the two primary temptations the young man faces. Further, this perspective helps us to see why passages about promiscuity always feature the seductive female rather than the lusty, aggressive male. As the passages are addressed to young men, they present females as tempters. Had the texts been addressed to young women, the picture of the role of males in initiating sexual relationships would have been entirely different. Both the preacher and the congregation must recognize this if they are to assimilate these passages appropriately.

In preaching this passage, the pastor will want to preserve in some manner the protasis-apodosis pattern that governs the text itself. The preacher may find a creative and original way to do this, but it may be just as well to preach a sermon that follows the structure of the passage in a fairly straightforward manner. In applying the text to a modern congregation, the pastor will need to include other applications alongside of those provided in verses 12–19. To older men and women in business, the message may stress how heeding wisdom and the Word of God keeps people from entering shady business relationships. To younger women, the message may stress how wisdom will keep them from the wrong kind of men. But the original thrust of the passage, the temptation to gangs and to easy sex, should not be neglected. A casual look at modern culture tells us that violent gangs and promiscuity are still major problems for urban young men.

A second wisdom poem to look at is Proverbs 31:10–31, the song in praise of the virtuous woman. A casual glance might suggest that this text, at least, is written primarily for women and not for men, but a close inspection reveals that this is not so. Some time ago I argued that the structure of this text is a fifteen-part chiasmus, as follows:[1]

A High value of a good wife (v. 10)
  B Husband benefited by wife (vv. 11–12)
    C Wife works hard (vv. 13–19)
      D Wife gives to poor (v. 20)
        E No fear of snow (v. 21a)
          F Children clothed in scarlet (v. 21b)
            G Coverings for bed, wife wears linen (v. 22)
              H Public respect for husband (v. 23)
            G′ Sells garments and sashes (v. 24)
          F′ Wife clothed in dignity (v. 25a)
        E′ No fear of future (v. 25b)
      D′ Wife speaks wisdom (v. 26)
    C′ Wife works hard (v. 27)
  B′ Husband and children praise wife (vv. 28–29)
A′ High value of a good wife (vv. 30–31)

The above structure is self-evidently a chiasmus (those who wish for further explication of the parallels indicated above should consult my commentary). What is most noteworthy here is the position of "H" at the hinge or pivot point of the chiasmus, verse 23, where the text abruptly speaks of how highly regarded is the woman's husband "at the gate" (that is, in the public square). Here alone, the virtuous woman does not appear at all. What is going on in this verse? Often, the hinge or pivot section at the center of a chiasmus is critical for interpretation. It tells us what is really the point of the whole text. Now it seems certain that the point here is *not* that the reason the woman is industrious, wise, and kind is because she is married to an important man. Rather, the man is highly regarded by his peers *because he has such a great wife*. In short, by placing the honored husband at the center of the poem, the text is telling the young man: "If you want to succeed and be well thought of, marry this kind of woman!" In other words, this passage is addressed to the young man and tells him what qualities to look for in a wife. Physical beauty, a playful personality, and other attributes that a man may seek in a woman are all secondary; the most important matter is that she fears God and has strong character.

In preaching the passage, of course, the pastor would not want to address only the unmarried males in the congregation. Just as the text encourages men concerning what kind of woman to seek out, it should also instruct women (for example, that godliness is more important than being up-to-date with all the latest fashion). This text can also address the issue of women working outside the home (see v. 24). And of course, the virtues of the woman of this passage—diligence, fidelity, compassion, and piety—should be developed by all people.

The structure of Proverbs 31:10–31 also shows us that sometimes the structure of the text cannot be repeated in the structure of the sermon. A chiastic sermon with fifteen points would be impossible to follow. A well-crafted sermon should faithfully relate what the text teaches without necessarily reproducing its outline.

Collections of Aphorisms

The preaching of the aphorism section of Proverbs (that is, the proverb collections in chapters 10–30) is notoriously difficult. How, after all, is one to develop a sermon based on a passage where every verse is a self-contained proverb that may or may not have any connection to its neighbors? A sermon that simply commented on each proverb in sequence would be at the least tedious and at the worst bewildering to a congregation. Such a sermon would only reinforce the impression that Proverbs has no order to it at all.

One common solution is to preach a series that collects proverbs on related themes. There are proverbs on laziness (10:4, 5, 26; 12:24, 27; 13:4; 15:19; 18:9), on drunkenness (20:1; 21:17; 23:20–21, 29–35; 31:4–7), on how wickedness leads to death (10:25, 27;

11:7, 10; 13:9; 14:32; 21:16), and on many other varied topics. One could thus have a kind of *Nave's Topical Bible* approach to sermon preparation and seek out texts from all over Proverbs that deal with single issues. Doing this, however, only raises the question of why the Bible itself does not group proverbs by topics and instead presents them in a seemingly random fashion.

It is possible, however, that the proverbs of Proverbs 10–30 are not nearly as random as they appear to be. The first clue is found in passages where two or more proverbs that obviously have bearing on one another are set side-by-side. A classic example is Proverbs 26:4–5, here cited in the NRSV:

> Do not answer fools according to their folly,
> or you will be a fool yourself.
> Answer fools according to their folly,
> or they will be wise in their own eyes.

Plainly, these two proverbs are on the surface contradictory of one another and give conflicting advice. Which one is correct? The answer, of course, is that both are correct. Sometimes one must answer fools according to their folly (with shouting, sarcasm, berating, and so forth) because that is the only language that they understand. A sergeant does not get through to a group of lazy, ignorant recruits with polite suggestions. On the other hand, speaking in this manner can get to be a habit, and the person who does so may soon be as pigheaded as those he shouts at. Neither proverb gives the whole picture. Together, they tell us that sometimes harsh speech is necessary but that the use of such language endangers the speaker himself.

Examples like Proverbs 26:4–5 suggest that there may be many such collections in Proverbs where each individual verse is true of itself but that, if read as part of a collection, it is seen to be a part of a much larger teaching in which new facets and levels of meaning appear. Discovering such collections in Proverbs is difficult; I have made tentative efforts in this direction with my commentary on Proverbs.[2] These collections, I believe, come together in various ways: some follow a common theme, some have a parallel or chiastic structure, some use repetition of a word or phrase (as in "Do not answer a fool . . . / Answer a fool . . . " in Prov. 26:4–5), and there are other devices as well. The main point is that in such a collection the whole is greater than the sum of the parts.

As an example, we can look at the very first proverb collection after the wisdom poems: Proverbs 10:1–5. The text reads (NIV):

> The proverbs of Solomon:
> A wise son brings joy to his father,
>   but a foolish son grief to his mother.
> Ill-gotten treasures are of no value,
>   but righteousness delivers from death.
> The LORD does not let the righteous go hungry
>   but he thwarts the craving of the wicked.
> Lazy hands make a man poor,
>   but diligent hands bring wealth.
> He who gathers crops in summer is a wise son,
>   but he who sleeps during harvest is a disgraceful son.

The theme of the passage is economic security—the fact that we all want to avoid poverty. In verse 1, we read that a son, by his wisdom or folly, brings joy or grief to his parents. In verse 5, we learn how to tell the one kind of son from the other: the wise son works hard to bring in a harvest, while the foolish son is lazy. Verse 2 warns against a wrong way of seeking economic security, through crime or corrupt behavior (taking bribes, cheating in business dealings, and so forth). Verse 4, by contrast, speaks of the right way to achieve prosperity, by hard work. At the middle of it all, in verse 3, the text tells us that the Lord watches over the righteous and will not let them fall into poverty. What do we make of all of this?

- Prosperity is rooted in the values of the family. Those who practice and teach a strong work ethic will do well (vv. 1, 5).
- The family is an interdependent body, with the strong or weak character of its individual members affecting all other members for good or ill (vv. 1, 5).

- Many seek shortcuts to prosperity, but these end in disaster (v. 2).
- The maxim that success and prosperity are best attained by hard work and honesty remains true (v. 4).
- Above everything else, security is attained by a pious walk before God. After all, no matter how hard we work or how strong our values are, disaster can always overtake us. We are secure only when we know that we are worth more than many sparrows and that God is our hope and protection (Matt. 10:29–31).
- At the same time, the fact that our hope is in God does not undermine the need for strong family values and a good work ethic. We cannot use piety as an excuse for laziness (2 Thess. 3:6–13).

Recognizing that these five verses form a structural whole enables us to proclaim a message on prosperity and security that encompasses many insights. Proverbs contains many collections such as this.

Preaching Psalms

The preaching of psalms is in principle the same as the preaching of wisdom poems except that, as described above, some psalms are too long for a single sermon and some are more complex than the average wisdom poem. A few examples, beyond those already given, should suffice to illustrate the preaching of psalms.

Psalm 23 is, of course, the most famous psalm of all. Despite its brevity, however, it is surprisingly complex. It has virtually none of the parallelism we have been trained to look for in Hebrew poetry (the only two lines that are arguably parallel are in verse 2), and the lines have highly irregular length. Thus, we will not find a parallel or chiastic structure here. What we do have, simply enough, is two governing metaphors: the Lord as shepherd (vv. 1–4) and the Lord as host (vv. 5–6). This division is very important, however; many a preacher has erred by trying to explain the entire text under the image of shepherd and sheep. But verses 5–6 concern a guest at a banquet, as in Matthew 22:1–14. In Psalm 23:5, the table is simply a table—it is not a "tableland" for sheep (the word is never used that way in the Old Testament). The ancients put oil on the heads of their guests, not of their sheep (there is no evidence for such a practice among ancient shepherds). People, not sheep, drink from cups. The point here is that in proclaiming Psalm 23, we need to preach both images and not just one. Jesus is both the good shepherd and the host of the great feast.

Another familiar passage, Psalm 1, also divides into two major sections, giving in this instance two contrasting parallels. The first half, verses 1–3, describes the qualities and fate of the righteous while the second half, verses 4–6, describes the fate of the wicked. Contrasting agricultural metaphors, the fruit tree by the waters of verse 3 over against the chaff driven in the wind of verse 4, point out the permanence and vitality of the righteous over against the transience and death of the wicked.

An entirely different kind of psalm is Psalm 125, a "Psalm of Ascent," but it also has two major divisions. The first part, verses 1–3, is an exposition of how the people of God are like Jerusalem. Like Jerusalem, or at least like the ideal that Jerusalem represents, they will abide forever and never be under the domain of evil. The second part, verses 4–5, is a prayer for such people and for Israel. May God watch over and keep them, the true inhabitants of the city of God! It is striking that we have a kind of eschatological assertion of the purity of the people of God coupled to a prayer that they actually be sustained as the people of God. One might proclaim this text with an eye on New Testament teaching that the church is, on the one hand, a pure virgin before God, but that on the other hand it is a corruptible human institution ever in need of our prayers.

Other Issues in Preaching Poetry

This essay has focused on the structure of poetic and wisdom passages and the bearing that has on interpretation and proclamation. There are other important issues, however, that we will briefly touch upon.

Form Criticism and Preaching

Every seminary student has some familiarity with form criticism and the psalms. Some psalms are described as "hymns" (community songs of praise), others as "communal laments" (community prayers for help), and others as "individual songs of thanksgiving" (sung by one person rather than a whole community), or "individual laments," "royal songs," "Torah psalms," and so forth. It is important to know these categories insofar as they force us to ask ourselves, "Was this psalm for one person or a whole congregation?" "Is this psalm a prayer to God, or is it addressed to the reader?" "Is this reflecting a celebration or a calamity?" Although form criticism has its value, and in some instances is extremely helpful, on the whole I am not persuaded that it is of great use to the preacher. It is a tool, but no more.

Meter in Hebrew Poetry

Some commentaries devote a good deal of attention to demonstrating what the commentary author believes to be the meter of each psalm. Most who follow this method believe that Hebrew poetry was built around a pattern of stressed syllables. In such commentaries, you will see lines of psalms described as having "3+3" meter, "3+2" meter, or some other quantity. For myself, I doubt that meter existed in Hebrew poetry and more strongly believe that if it did exist, we have not yet figured out how it worked. The preacher, in my opinion, should disregard references to meter in commentaries on the psalms.

Messianic Psalms

Any kind of psalm ("individual psalm of lament" or "royal psalm," for instance) can have a messianic aspect. Psalms 2 and 45 ("royal psalms") and Psalm 22 (an "individual psalm of lament") are all heavily messianic. Thus, the preacher should not assume that there is a single category of "messianic psalms" but be prepared for messianic significance in all kinds of psalms. We have, in this brief essay, noted messianic aspects of Psalm 23 (a "psalm of trust"); there is also some messianic import in the "city of God" motif of Psalm 125. It is essential to see, however, that these psalms continue to function both within the Old Testament and as pointers toward the New Testament. On the one hand, Psalm 23 describes the trust of David in the God of Israel. On the other hand, Psalm 23 is perfectly fulfilled in Jesus. The preacher should not allow one aspect of the psalm to obscure the other.

Questions to Consider

1. What role does the structure of a psalm play in determining its meaning?
2. What is the function of chiasm in psalms or proverbs?
3. How does meter function in psalms?
4. Reflect on how you can take the tips from this chapter and put them into practice in your sermon preparation. What's your plan?

On the Shelf

Bullock, C. Hassel. *Encountering the Book of Psalms: A Literary and Theological Introduction*. Grand Rapids: Baker, 2004.

Garrett, Duane A. *Proverbs, Ecclesiastes, and Song of Songs*. New American Commentary 14. Nashville: Broadman Press, 1993.

Kidner, Derek. *Psalms 1–72* and *Psalms 73–150*. Tyndale Old Testament Commentaries. Downers Grove, IL: InterVarsity Press, 1981.

Lewis, C. S. *Reflections on the Psalms*. Glasgow: Collins, 1961.

Weiser, Artur. *The Psalms: A Commentary*. Translated by Herbert Hartwell. London: SCM Press, 1962.

7

Preaching from the Prophets

John H. Sailhamer

Preparing to preach from the prophets involves many of the same issues dealt with in other parts of this book.[1] These are usually grouped around headings such as hermeneutical, exegetical, theological, and homiletical. Along with those issues, the task of preaching from the prophets has its own unique problems. The underlying question of my discussion is whether or not the message of the Old Testament prophets in its present form as Scripture is as "preachable" as the New Testament gospel and, if so, how one should identify this message as such within the prophetic writings.

Thoughts on the Question: Who are the "Prophets"?

Though there are many ways such a subject might be approached, the fact that the prophetic writings come to us as inspired Scripture (2 Tim. 3:16) obliges us to take seriously their final written form and to strive all the more to understand them as a function of the meaning of a "book." It is our contention that when viewed from the perspective of the prophets as authors, it is possible to see in their books a line of thought already moving in the same theological direction as the New Testament books themselves. That is to say that in the composition of the prophetic books, one can already detect a development of the gospel and the "new covenant" identical in most respects to the gospel Jesus preached (Luke 22:20; Rom. 16:25–26). This was long before the coming of Christ. From such a vantage point there is considerable agreement between what it means to preach from the prophets and to preach from the New Testament. Both involve understanding texts and both are basically exegetical in nature. Most importantly, both turn on the same theological foci that form the basis of a Christian theology: covenant blessing, faith, and law, to mention only three. This suggests that by the time of the completion of the Old Testament Canon (Tanakh), many or all of the central New Testament themes had already played themselves out in full measure within the books of the Old Testament themselves.

Thus the notion of a "prophetic book," which first rose to prominence in the "making" of the canonical "book of Moses" (Dan. 9:10), carries with it unavoidable implications for preaching from the prophets. For example, with the rise of the prophetic "book," long-standing religious ideals and yearnings in Israel, such as knowing God's will and experiencing his presence, came increasingly to be mediated through Scripture rather than more traditional religious structures such as the temple and the priesthood. In spite of their deep roots in the religious heritage of ancient Israel, internal evidence of the theological nature of the structure of the Hebrew Bible as a whole (Tanakh) suggests that such institutions were rapidly being replaced by a new emphasis on the individual as a reader who meditates on Scripture "as a book."[2]

Reading the Bible had itself become an act of worship (Nehemiah 8). As we have suggested elsewhere,[3] the "making" of the Bible into a book was not a gradual and nebulous literary-historical process but was rather a real historical act that occurred in a moment of time not unlike the historical events recounted in the Bible itself. History, as such, had become a way of experiencing divine reality and spiritual truth on an individual level, particularly as that history was recounted by the Bible as experienced by individuals. Hence, in "making the Bible a book," the biblical authors, having gathered the necessary source materials, set out to render their thoughts through words alone and to put them down to be read in meaningful portions. Being competent in such matters, the biblical authors followed time-honored, though ancient, methods of "composition," rendering their writings still today accessible to historical analysis as written texts (philology).

In turning to the ancient art of "making" books, the biblical prophets managed to forge a powerful new weapon by which to hurl their words against the walls of irreligion and hypocrisy—that is, the weapon of the written word. If left without their books and their written words, the biblical prophets had only their voices and their sometimes inexplicable actions (Isaiah 20). At an early stage they had discovered that books gave them considerably more intellectual leverage than their actions, which always had to be explained and interpreted. The ability to render one's thoughts in a book also gave the prophets a new, and thus far untried, means of theological reflection. This was more than a mere extension of the power of the pen. It also meant that the prophets' words could be placed alongside the words of other biblical writers and even alongside the words of God as a way of giving his divine utterances depth and context. Making books meant that anyone, whether within earshot of a prophet or not, could "hear" the prophets' words and read them diligently, again and again, so that they might be reflectively passed on to others. The making of prophetic books meant that God's words, once received, could be given a context and setting that transcended particular moments in time.

Once the task of "making" a book had become, for the prophet, the central focus of his act of preaching, his message, though it never really changed, also never again remained exactly the same. Some point to a "democratization" of the prophetic Word. God's Word, the sole possession of the prophet, was put into the hand of anyone desiring and able to read a book.[4] The scope assumed by the prophetic "books" was broad enough to include the king and the priests. According to Deuteronomy 17, the king was required to write out a copy of "the Torah" in "a book" and to use it in the administration of his kingdom. Its purpose was to enable him to "read it all the days of his life" (Deut. 17:18–20). As a "book of Moses" (Torah), Scripture had become a kind of Magna Carta to whose authority even the king and priest were to submit, thereby defining the spiritual responsibility of both offices in terms of its own prophetic vision. Even the words of the prophets, which had yet to take their place in a book, had to be judged authentic by conforming to what was written in "the Torah and the Testimony."[5] In Isaiah 2:2–4, a world is envisioned "in the last days" in which the nations will come to the temple, not to receive its benefits as a temple (namely, the priesthood and sacrifices), but to study and be taught the prophetic Word (Torah). The obvious implication of this crucial passage is that the temple was to become a house of learning, that is, a place to study the Scriptures. By means of the Torah that was to come out of Zion, the Lord will judge the nations. The result is that the nations will "hammer their swords into plowshares, and their spears into pruning hooks. Nation will not lift up sword against nation, and never again will they learn war" (Isa. 2:4 NASB).

Moreover, in those biblical texts that serve as canonical links between the major sections of the Hebrew Bible (Josh. 1:8; Ps. 1:2), the goal of becoming wise and being successful in life is viewed in terms of meditation on the Torah as a "book." Readers of Scripture are to meditate on the Bible by reading it as a "book." There they will find godly wisdom (Josh. 1:8) and success (Ps. 1:2). The importance of these texts lies in the fact that they are a central part of the canonical glue that binds together the Old Testament Canon (Tanakh). These and other programmatic texts (see Deut. 4:6) identify biblical wisdom as the written prophetic Word of Scripture. In this they are very much like the editorial comment in the subscript of the book of Hosea (14:9 NASB). They identify the prophetic writings not as the proclamation of divine judgment but as lessons in "biblical wisdom":

> Whoever is wise, let him understand these things;
> Whoever is discerning, let him know them.
> For the ways of the LORD are right,
> And the righteous will walk in them,
> But transgressors will stumble in them.

Given such an emphasis on the written Scriptures in the prophetic tradition, understanding the prophets as authors of books, rather than merely proclaimers of divine judgment and salvation in particular social settings, should be the central focus of the question of preaching from the prophets. Such a focus may require some adjustment to our thinking, particularly if we have in mind the question of preaching the prophetic books to New Testament believers. Above all it will require a greater sensitivity to the notion of the prophetic word as something contained in an inspired book[6] and not merely something proclaimed to an ancient audience. Along with that, as far as the prophets are now concerned, it will require our paying attention to the notion that the prophets now speak to us both as the authors of their books and as narrative characters within the framework of those books (see Jeremiah 36). This means that understanding the prophets entails, among other things, being a good reader. That is a way of saying we must be aware of such bookish kinds of things as plot, characterization, thematic structure, and compositional strategy.

Above all it will mean being aware of one's complete dependence on the author of the books we are reading. Such things are the stuff of the prophetic message that has come down to us. It is through understanding such features that one comes to an understanding of what and how to preach from the prophets. Preaching the prophets is more than repeating the prophets' words in new and different settings. Understanding and preaching the prophets requires that we be competent readers who know how to understand a book and the meaning of its author. In many cases it also means being able to preach someone else's sermon. As Heschel has argued, understanding the prophets is often a matter of an exegesis of an exegesis. The prophets' books are not mere anthologies of previously recorded versions of their sermons. The prophets' books are their sermons, delivered in book form. Our task is to preach their books.

Reading the prophets as a book also means not confusing the intended reader of the prophetic books with the audiences of the ancient prophets. The prophets did not distribute their words to Israel in bound copies. Their words were heard, remembered, and explained, primarily as they became part of a book. While a prophet's primary task was to confront the ungodly with words of warning, the primary task of the prophetic books was to give comfort to those who read them. That comfort came in the reassurance of God's faithfulness to his "new covenant" promises. That is what the prophetic authors intended to give to their readers as a basis for their continued hope. Preaching from the prophets ultimately means extending the range of their biblical sermons about the "new covenant" to include the church audience.

Such an understanding of the prophets opens many doors to preaching the prophets in, and to, the church. While the substance of much of the prophets' warnings is the Sinai covenant, the actual message of the prophetic books centers on the "new covenant."[7] In other words, the prophetic books, as books, have the same theological purpose as the books of the New Testament. They speak of God's continuous commitment to his covenant pledge to bless Israel and the nations by means of a "new" covenant (Gen. 12:1–3). The mediator of that pledge is the "seed of Abraham" (Gen. 22:18; Gal. 3:16). God's means of accomplishing his pledge is to inscribe the divine law upon the hearts of all believers. The prophets did not write their books to teach their readers the Sinai covenant. Their intent, like Moses's, was to call their readers to a life of faith under the new covenant (Isa. 7:9b).

There is considerable evidence suggesting the authors of the prophetic books were familiar with the earliest books of the Bible, including the Mosaic Pentateuch. Anyone who has read the prophetic books knows that they have drawn heavily from the Pentateuch. In doing so they have clarified and given depth to its message. It is also evident from reading the writings of other prophetic authors that they too drew heavily from prophetic books other than the Pentateuch. As those who had diligently studied the Mosaic Scriptures, the authors of the later prophetic books saw themselves primarily as exegetes of the words of the earlier prophets, including the Pentateuch. Just as Moses drew heavily from his exegesis of the ancient sources available to him in "making" the Pentateuch, the prophetic authors depended largely on their exegesis of the Pentateuch and earlier prophetic Scriptures[8] for their understanding of the Word. These prophets, functioning as expository preachers, aimed at providing a biblical context for the rest of Scripture by tying it to their exegesis of the Pentateuch. They were in effect doing what we would today call biblical exposition.

The meaning of prophetic books in general came thus to be grounded in the pages of earlier, more ancient, Scriptures, which were themselves founded on the book of Moses. Each passage echoed the word of another. Hosea, for example, sketched his messianic vision from a close reading of Numbers 23 and 24. He saw from his own exegesis of the Pentateuch, which today can still be retraced, that it had envisioned the Messiah as a new Moses and a future king from the house of Judah.[9] It was such prophets who kept the interest in the "book of Moses" alive (Dan. 9:10)—often in spite of centuries of neglect. It is ultimately to these prophets that we owe the composition of the Old Testament in the first place. In their dependence on the Pentateuch and the connections they drew to it, the words of the prophetic books were every bit the picture of what Hengstenberg once called a prophetic "echo." As Ernst Wilhelm Hengstenberg described it, a prophetic echo is a way of picturing the prophet's efforts to keep the Word of God alive and relevant by recasting it in new and more profound ways. As the prophets listened to the words of Moses in the Pentateuch, they responded with words of their own.[10] Their words were explanatory and as such were intended to probe the text with questions. This meant their personal understanding of their faith often took on the character of a "biblical" theology.

For these prophetic authors, biblical "books" were more than relics of the past. These ancient books that eventually found their way into the Old Testament Canon were, instead, the very means by which their faith was nourished. When Moses, by means of a strategic use of biblical poetry, identified the promised seed of Abraham (Gen. 22:18) as an individual king from the house of Judah (Gen. 49:8–12), he was laying down a compositional foundation later identified and picked up by Jeremiah (4:2) and the Psalms (72:17) as a way of identifying the coming messianic king.

How far back did this prophetic biblicism extend? The preceding example suggests it reached as far back as Moses. Not only was he the author of the first biblical book, the Pentateuch, but, given the prophetic echoes within the Pentateuch, Moses might also be seen as the prototypical prophetic author. Such prophetic authors continued to link Moses to their future hope in such a way that it led ultimately to the "new covenant" message being passed on to the New Testament.

Returning to our initial question, Who were the prophets whose message we are to preach? Our answer is that they are the prophetic authors of the biblical prophetic books whose message is grounded in the book of Moses and whose vision looks forward to the "new covenant" gospel of faith. If that is a proper aim, there would seem to be little that stands in the way of the Christian's preaching from the Old Testament prophets.

Must We also Preach the Sermons the Prophets Preached in Their Own Times?

The relevance of the prophets' sermons in the church is an open question, yet few today would dare preach a message like Amos 2:4–5 (my translation):

> Because of three rebellions of Judah, and because of four, I will not return him. Because they rejected the Torah (Law) of the LORD and did not keep his statutes; their lies (idols), after which their fathers walked, led them astray; and I will send fire against Judah and it will consume the citadel of Jerusalem.

The practice of preaching a "prophetic" sermon of judgment and divine retribution like Amos's has been a trademark of many "biblical" preachers. Famous preachers, such as Billy Sunday, have been known to model their sermons on those of the biblical prophets, focusing not only on the gospel, but also on warnings of divine judgment.

In addition to such sermons, there is also a further sense in which preaching the prophets has come to mean taking one's stand against social evils and political corruption. Such prophetic models have earned an honorable place in the contemporary preacher's repertoire. But what such sermons underscore is not the basic similarity between the biblical prophets and today's preachers but their vast differences. Does not the prophetic model of preaching God's Word to our world call for a fundamental change in the prophetic message? Are we justified in preaching the sermons of the prophets in the church if it means the misapplication of their message to a different context? Although many evangelicals would grant a place for such prophetic preaching, most would do so only after adding numerous cautionary words.

In the last analysis, one must remember that there is a genuine difference between the ancient prophets' message in its context and our preaching that message today. It is as much a societal and political difference as it is a theological one. The problem, of course, is where one locates that difference. Every preacher must decide individually where to draw the line. On this issue though we might do well to heed the example of Walter Kaiser's work on the prophets. While Kaiser has steadfastly refused to silence the prophets, he also repeatedly warns against giving them the last word. While he might prefer to let the prophets speak for themselves, he has learned also never to let them hold the microphone.

Kaiser's answer to the question of whether the prophets' message can be reproduced as a statement of the gospel to the church lies in the nature of his understanding of the prophetic word. As his starting point, Kaiser rejects the notion that the biblical prophets addressed their sermons to social structures and institutions, arguing instead that the prophets addressed the nation as a whole only on the basis of an individual appeal. Their message was always that of personal salvation. It would be a mistake, Kaiser argues, to see the prophets as precursors of twenty-first century revolutionaries rallying the masses and calling for social change on a grand scale. On the contrary, he insists, throughout their public ministries, the prophets always directed their messages to individuals, offering them not so much a change in their collective physical and political environment as, personally and individually, a change in their heart. In doing so, the possibility of a change in societal structures as a result of a change of heart was an item left open to a future work of God. Thus Kaiser concludes:

> That the prophets addressed themselves primarily to individuals in their attempt to effect massive changes in society (whether those individuals were judges, other government officials, merchants, or clergy) gives us a clue as to how we might proclaim their message anew in our day. But simply to redirect their message to contemporary men and women is not sufficient in and of itself. It will not help the interpreter/proclaimer merely to state that there is some type of connection between the ancient and modern audience.[11]

The Sermon of the "Prophetic Author"

Recent studies in the prophetic literature tend to confirm Kaiser's observations on the individual presentation of the prophet and his sermon. Such studies focus both on the point of view of the ancient prophet and his call to confront the evils of his countrymen, as well as the legacy of such prophets as preserved through the process of their "making" a prophetic book.[12] Though one may dispute whether Israel's prophets were called to confront their countrymen individually, a close reading of their books shows that this is exactly what those authors did. The prophetic authors took great care to cast their message in individual terms. It is important to note that this feature of the prophetic message can be argued exegetically, not from "shreds" of reconstructed "pre-history" that critical scholars claim to have "discovered" behind every prophetic utterance, but, more importantly, on the basis of two larger observations that hold true in many individual examples from the prophetic writings.

The first is the theological direction indicated in these prophetic books by the compositional strategy of their authors. These are authors both in the traditional sense and in terms of the canonical task of putting together the whole of the Old Testament Tanakh and glossing it with admonitions to "meditate on these texts day and night" in order to gain, not a new revolutionary society, but personal "wisdom" and "understanding" in living one's life before God (Joshua 1; Psalm 1). Such notices are not scattered randomly throughout the Tanakh, nor do they appear to be targeted specifically at social institutions and power structures as such. They are rather presented in terms of a broad distributional pattern that follows the contours of the compositional structure of the books themselves, suggesting anyone and everyone may "read and take heed" of them. In a word, by targeting individual readers, the Canon as such (Tanakh) suggests that its understanding of the prophetic word has the same focus as Kaiser argues for the prophet and his individual message.

The second observation centers on those texts that represent the prophets as ministers of a "new covenant" distinct from Sinai (Deut. 28:69 [29:1]; Jer. 31:31). These texts betray the presence of biblical authors whose ideas are close to those behind the final shape of the Old Testament. Such "new covenant" signatures include the individualization of the pledge to receive a "new heart" (Ezekiel 36), internalization of the Torah by having it written on one's heart (Jeremiah 31), and the role of the Spirit in rendering the new heart obedient to God's will as expressed in the prophetic books (Neh. 9:20). It is not merely possible but quite likely that one could sketch out a comprehensive program of preaching the Old Testament prophets by following these "new covenant" strategies throughout the prophetic literature. Such lines of thought point one to similar compositional strategies that lead directly into the New Testament (cf. Hebrews 8).[13] The prophetic "faith theme" (*Glaubens Thematik*), which Han-Christoph Schmitt traced throughout the Pentateuch and Old Testament, is also marked by its association with the compositional strategies of individual prophetic books (Isaiah, for example). Those same strategies reappear in New Testament books such as the Gospel of John (John 20:30) and the book of Hebrews (chap. 11) and often include a focus on a coming "messianic" king.[14] These texts show that the "prophetic books," as the inscripturated messages of the prophets, confront the individual in such a way that they present themselves as mediators of a "new covenant." What these initial observations suggest is that by means of the process of "book making," the message of the ancient prophets has been refitted to serve a new life setting, one that focuses the reader's attention on an individual reading and meditation on Scripture as the means of finding divine blessing and wisdom. In such a "new covenant" environment, the "new heart" is presented as something to be nourished by God's Word and given life and growth by the "Spirit." Such thoughts are unmistakably like the pattern for the church in Ephesians 4.

Abraham Heschel[15] once suggested that there are always at least two sermons in a prophetic text. There is the sermon that the prophet preached in his own times and to his own contemporaries, and there is the sermon the author of a prophetic book preaches by means of his book. There is the "sermon *of* the prophet," and there is the "sermon *about* the prophet." The prophet's sermon was a divine word to his own generation. It is not the message of the prophetic book to our day. On the other hand, the prophetic author's sermon, which comes to us not in, but as, the prophetic book, is directed to anyone who reads the book. That is what the Canon is about. The sermon *of* the prophet is about the divine response to Israel's straying from God. The sermon *about* the prophet is the result of the biblical author's reflections and interpretation of the prophet's words. It comes to us as a prophetic book whose presentation is about the prophet and his words. The prophet's sermon comes from his divine call to go out to the people and proclaim the words God has given him. The biblical author's sermon is a function of his collecting the prophet's words and putting them into a book. The biblical prophet "makes" his sermon from the word given him by God. The biblical author "makes" his sermon by "making" a book out of the biblical prophet's words.

The sermon of the prophet Jonah consisted of only five Hebrew words, "In yet forty days Nineveh will be destroyed" (Jon. 3:4).[16] The sermon of the *book* of Jonah consists of the meaning of the rest of the book's 705 words. The task of preaching the book of Jonah lies not in repeating Jonah's five-word sermon to members of the church. The sermon of the prophetic author of the book of Jonah consists of his "making" the rest of the book that proclaims a "new covenant" in the events of the book. The "new covenant" meaning of the book can be seen in its focus, not on God's judgment of Jonah (Jonah 1) and Nineveh (Jonah 4), but on God's grace to the Gentile sailors and Ninevites in chapters 1 and 3 along with Jonah's selfish ingratitude toward God's gracious treatment of the Gentiles (Jon. 4:11). Jonah's words to Nineveh are threats of divine judgment. The book's word to its readers is a call to faith. The book reminds us that the Gentile Ninevites "believed God" (Jon. 3:5) just as Abraham did in the Genesis narratives (Gen. 15:6).

Both Jonah, the prophet, and the prophetic author of the book of Jonah have their words to speak in this book. Jonah's five words to Nineveh are a small and almost incidental part of the rest of the words of the prophet's book. In that book, the prophetic author has written a gospel of faith stressing the new covenant hope of the salvation of the Gentiles. The prophet Jonah's message of judgment to Nineveh (Jon. 3:4b) provides the context for that word of faith. It is the message of the book of Jonah as a whole that presents the word of faith and divine grace. To be sure, we should take the five words of Jonah as the words of God, but we should remember that it is also the additional 705 inspired words of the book's prophetic author that make the book of Jonah part of our Holy Scriptures and the subject of our preaching from the prophets. On the pages of the book of Jonah, both Jonah and his book stand before us, but only his book now speaks to us. We needn't today try to preach Jonah's sermon that "forty more days and Nineveh will be overturned." That prophetic word has no more place in our preaching than those of Amos to his generation noted above. As the apostle Paul sometimes puts it, "Scripture says . . ." (Rom. 9:17)—that is, Jonah's book as an exhortative narrative of the importance of Gentile faith still speaks to us today, just as Jonah once spoke to Nineveh. In the book of Jonah, the Scriptures curiously take on the role of the prophet himself, who speaks God's Word through the book. Reading a prophetic book like Jonah means treating each passage of Scripture as if it were the prophet himself speaking God's Word to us. That is what Christopher Seitz has called "letting a text 'act like a man.'"[17] As Scripture, the book itself comes to us as the prophet with a message to its reader and to our congregations. We know that message by reading the book.

What we are saying here about the book of Jonah applies equally to all biblical prophetic books. They, like the poems and narratives in the Pentateuch, render a message of divine truth and grace. They show us how to live "before God," and how to respond to his wondrous gift of grace and the Spirit. They also put before us the exegetical responsibility of understanding narratives and their compositional strategies.

Compositional Strategy of the Prophetic Book

If we are to treat a prophetic book "like a man," how do we get him to talk? More precisely, how do we get him to talk in a way we can understand? Are not the prophets we meet in these books often hard to understand? The brevity of their words, their minimal literary context, and the obscure imagery they use leave us sometimes with little more than a "sound bite" describing an event or an idea about which we know very little. Adding to the obscurity that often accompanies the prophets' words are their frequent use of ancient and rare vocabulary and the almost complete lack of historical context in their writings. How, for example, are we to understand the saying of Isaiah 28:10?

> command for-command, command for-command, line for-line, line for-line, little there, little there.[18]

A further aspect of the difficulty of the prophets no doubt lies in the poetic nature of their original words. Biblical poetry is inherently obscure, though that is not to say it is not also capable of great powers of description. But even nonpoetic passages, such as the "flying scroll" narrative in Zechariah 5:1–3, leave one little to go on for explanation.

The answer to these questions of meaning lies in gaining an appreciation of the purpose of the compositional strategy of the prophetic books. As we have suggested above, one can understand a compositional strategy as a plan or structure that ties the various parts of a book together into a whole. It is a way of making sense of a book's pieces by showing how the author has fit them into a larger whole.[19] The notion of such a strategy can also provide clues that enable one to retrace the work of the author to show the book's interconnections, or internal links, to other parts of the book and other parts of the Old Testament Canon (Tanakh). An awareness of such connections can give us a sense of the meaning of the whole of both a prophetic book and the Old Testament Canon. Granting that the biblical authors had an intent and desired to make that intention known through their books, the central task of the interpreter of the prophetic books becomes that of making sense of the parts of a book in terms of the meaning of the whole. Making sense of a prophetic book is not that different from putting a sermon together. One starts with a "big idea" and shapes the whole of the book around that idea or theme. The notion of a strategy or intelligent design lying behind a book helps us see where the author is going in the book and what the book is about. One can say that the author's book, as an expression of his own identity and religious faith, begins to take on the personality of the author and can almost be said to "think" or "act like the author." We the readers of the book can interact with the author of the book the same way we would interact with a person who wants to tell us something about himself and his faith in God.

These kinds of interconnections help us see the development of the prophetic author's meaning in his book, and they can be described both internally and externally. The internal connections of a book (innertextuality) are the primary way that the larger themes of a book are developed. The external links of a prophetic book (intertextuality) enable us to see how the author of the book understands its relationship to other books in the Old Testament Canon. The author of the book of Isaiah, for example, spends a good deal of his time pointing to connections between his ideas and the ideas developed by Moses, the author of the Pentateuch. The author of the book of Isaiah wants his book to "act like" the prophet Isaiah, who in turn behaves like a second Moses. As one senses such interconnections, a way is opened to the larger context of understanding in the book of Isaiah, particularly against the background of the book of Moses. As Schmitt[20] has demonstrated, both the Pentateuch and the book of Isaiah are already written with a view to what was to become the New Testament notion of justification by faith. That theme continued to make itself known even at the heart of the formation of the New Testament (cf. John 20:31[21] and Hebrews 11).

A further difficulty of the prophets and their writings is the fact that in drawing out the interconnections of their books with other biblical books, they frequently draw on sometimes remote texts of Scripture and thus presuppose a kind of "biblical literacy" that is beyond the average Bible reader. At the conclusion of the prophecies of Hosea (14:9), the author warns his readers of the need for wisdom and understanding to comprehend Hosea's message (my translation):

> Whoever is wise, let him understand these things.
> And whoever is discerning let him know them—because the ways of the LORD are upright.
> The righteous walk in them, but the rebellious stumble in them.

This is not an encouraging word for modern readers who know they do not know as much as the prophet supposes. It raises the bar of understanding a prophetic book like Hosea far beyond the range of the modern reader. Who would want to say one has the requisite "wisdom" of which this passage speaks? Even if one had such "wisdom," how should it be used to understand the book? Would one's wisdom reveal a meaning that is not in the book, or would it make clearer and more applicable one that is already there? Fortunately we can understand the prophets and their books in general terms merely by paying close attention to the Pentateuch and the other prophetic books that make up the larger parts of the Old Testament Canon, even if we do not "get" all of the interconnections and allusions noted by the author. Knowing they are there, however, can open one to the experience of making a connection and thus sharing a kindred thought with the ancient author. Sharing such a thought in a sermon from the prophets makes for a long remembered moment of truth. In biblical terms, such a moment of truth is called an insight (*sekel*, Neh. 8:8, 13).

The Role of Historical Background in Understanding the Prophetic Text

Despite such well-known difficulties in understanding the prophets, there are some positive signs that preaching from biblical prophetic texts has a bright future. For many who study the Old Testament as ancient literature, the future of the prophetic literature lies in its past. As they see it, an understanding of ancient history and cultures opens new avenues into the meaning, or at least function, of the prophetic sermon. Biblical prophets are compared with their counterparts in the ancient world and, as is often the case, the differences, in both the content and the function of their message, are highlighted as an all-important key to the meaning of biblical prophecy. In such an approach, which is often historical and sociological rather than specifically exegetical, explanations have come to rival the importance of a close scrutiny of the text in determining the meaning of the prophetic word. As one evangelical Old Testament scholar has put it:

> Scholarship has sought to place the prophetic person and role within a wider social context. This involves locating prophets by noting the role they played in society in relation to other institutions, such as the monarchy and the priesthood. . . . This newer, sociological approach highlights the importance of the recipi-

> ents of the message in recognizing the messenger as a prophet, grounding his or her identity upon that recognition.[22]

In a way quite different from the traditional grammatical historical quest for the context of Israelite prophecy,[23] many scholars remain hopeful that an understanding of the historical circumstances of the prophets and their message will continue to provide essential clues to the meaning of these texts.

As we have attempted to demonstrate in this chapter, many have also begun to call for a closer examination of the biblical texts themselves as the most promising approach to preaching from the prophets. In recent years, biblical scholarship has turned to both the historical background of the prophets and the compositional nature of their writings as valuable guides to understanding both the prophets and their books. Such methodological interests, whether it be on the individual prophet or his book, can be focused on one of three areas: the "pre-history" of the prophet's message, the "historical context" of his message, and the "after-history" (*Nachgeschichte*) of the prophet's message.[24] American evangelicals have generally steered clear of the "pre-history" of the prophetic word, rightfully concerned that it often points away from the inspired text toward a reconstructed, hypothetical version of the prophet's message. I have in mind situations such as the distinction between the message of the prophet Isaiah and the critical reconstruction of a second prophet called Isaiah (Deutero-Isaiah) whose work was supposedly attached to the words of the eighth-century prophet by that same name.

The preferred approach of contemporary evangelical scholarship focuses its attention on preaching the prophet's message as it is understood within the context of the prophet's own historical setting. Sometimes that setting is given to the reader in the heading of the book, as in Hosea 1:1, for example. At other times the historical context must be restored to the text from hints and clues in the words of the prophet. The mention of the "Chaldeans" in Habakkuk 1:6, for example, can guide one's reading of the events of the book and Habakkuk's own words in terms of the historical context of the Babylonian invasion of

Jerusalem in the late sixth century. In speaking of this approach as it appeared in the nineteenth century, Milton Terry wrote:

> The interpreter should, therefore, endeavor to take himself from the present, and to transport himself into the historical position of his author, look through his eyes, note his surroundings, feel with his heart, and catch his emotion. Herein we note the import of the term grammatico-*historical* interpretation. We are not only to grasp the grammatical import of words and sentences, but also to feel the force and bearing of the historical circumstances which may in any way have affected the writer. . . . The individuality of the writer, his local surroundings, his wants and desires, his relation to those for whom he wrote, his nationality and theirs, the character of the times when he wrote—all these matters are of the first importance to a thorough interpretation of the several books of Scripture.[25]

Such a reconstruction of the "real" prophet from the historical setting of his book is the opposite of what Seitz means by "letting the text 'act like a man.'" The drawback is that it isolates the prophet's message in the past with few connections to the present and the role of the prophet's words in preaching. While such an approach may tell us much about what the prophet's message once meant to his hearers, it does little to help us understand how we might preach and apply that message to our day. It does not consider the question of the meaning of the text as such. As far as the evangelical is concerned, such an approach may also run the risk of elevating uninspired reconstructed historical events above the inspired biblical text (2 Tim. 3:16).

A Textual Approach to the Interpretation of Biblical Prophecy (After-History)

In recent years, considerable attention has been directed to the prophet's message as it comes to us in the form of a book.[26] That means a renewed interest in the "after-history"[27] of the prophetic word. The question of what happened to the prophet's message after he delivered it, both during his own lifetime and after, is of considerable interest in light of the fact that his words eventually made their way into a book about the prophet which we take to be inspired Scripture.[28] How does the "after-history" (*Nachgeschichte*) of the prophet's words help us understand and preach his message today? What effect on meaning does the process of becoming a book have on the prophet's words? I have suggested in this essay that asking such questions of meaning in this way has led to the realization that many of the interpretive problems one faces in preaching the prophet's message, such as the need for a proper context, have been addressed by the prophet in the process of "making" his words into a book and putting that book within a particular location in the Old Testament Canon. A book, such as those woven from the prophet's own words, can provide a valuable context for understanding and preaching those words.

What was said earlier about the Babylonian context given within the book of Habakkuk is a case in point. When reading the prophetic books one can expect that help is on the way from the author for a wide range of essential interpretive questions. The prophetic author is never far from the text itself and ready to supply a needed clue to the meaning of the prophet's sometimes obscure words. In a book such as we have from the prophets, help comes in the form of the intentional and meaningful compositional strategies employed by biblical prophetic authors. It may also come from an explanatory comment inserted by the author, within the text itself. As an authorial clue, and not merely a scribal gloss, such help comes to the reader with the highest authority. It is inspired Scripture. An example is the author's identification of the stump of the felled tree as "the holy seed" in Isaiah 6:13.

Conclusion

By way of conclusion, I offer a brief summary of the points argued in this chapter.

1. Evangelical approaches to preaching from the prophets have largely focused on two central objectives. The first is an

understanding of the ancient prophet and his message within his immediate social and historical context. The second is a focus on the message of the biblical authors who have given us the words of the ancient prophets in their inspired writings. Though these two views have rarely been held together, evangelical biblical scholarship cannot afford to lose its focus on either side. Limiting the prophet's message to what we might reconstruct of ancient Israelite faith and thought unduly restricts the meaning of the biblical prophets to past events and settings. Ultimately the question of preaching from the prophets turns on the message of the prophetic books. That leads to our second conclusion.

2. In the last analysis, the prophetic word that must be preached is that word which is presented to us in the prophetic writings. As important as historical reconstructions of a prophet's message are, the point at which the prophets must converge with the theology of the New Testament is at the level of the final compositional shape of the Hebrew Bible.

3. Preaching from the prophetic books means following the line of thought traversed by the author in the prophetic book and the "after-history" of that book. Knowing the prophetic message means recognizing it as it passes through, not only the remainder of the Old Testament, but also into the New Testament.

4. Without appearing to be too simplistic, we can say that the message of the Old Testament prophets, as embodied in their books, appears to be the same message as the New Testament writers. Though we must allow for some historical distance between the prophets themselves and our understanding of them today, it is clear that as a part of the prophetic literature, a biblical prophet's message, as embodied in his prophetic book, was the basis of the theology that we see in the New Testament. It is within the context of that theology we are to preach the prophets today.

Questions to Consider

1. What does it mean to be a good reader of the prophets?
2. In what way do the prophets target the individual reader?

3. What are the "new covenant signatures" and their implications for preaching?
4. What is the usefulness of a prophet's compositional strategy as it relates to preaching?
5. Reflect on how you can take the tips from this chapter and put them into practice in your sermon preparation. What's your plan?

On the Shelf

Kaiser, Walter C. *Malachi: God's Unchanging Love.* Grand Rapids: Baker, 1984.

Sailhamer, John H. *Biblical Prophecy.* Grand Rapids: Zondervan, 1998.

———. *The Pentateuch as Narrative: A Biblical-Theological Commentary.* Grand Rapids: Zondervan, 1992.

Schniedewind, William M. *How the Bible Became a Book.* Cambridge: Cambridge University Press, 2004.

8

Preaching the Old Testament in Light of Its Culture

Timothy S. Laniak

Evangelicals maintain a high regard for Scripture as divine revelation. We affirm God's ultimate authorship of the Canon. At the same time, we also appreciate its distinctly human character. The Bible is a library of separate books compiled by a variety of authors and editors over a long period of time. Each book reflects the particularity of its writers, intended audiences, and the countless contextually specific realities they shared. Centuries separate us from these realities. In more subtle ways vastly different cultural assumptions and perspectives contribute to this gap.

Occasionally evangelical sermons will illuminate the context of a passage of Scripture with reference to an extrabiblical text, archaeological discovery, or an anecdote from a recent trip to the Holy Land. With the help of resources like Walter C. Kaiser's *Hard Sayings of the Old Testament*[1] and others mentioned below, preachers can find straightforward explanations for troubling passages. Still, it must be admitted, anecdotes and illustrations from the world of the Bible are increasingly rare and are typically engaged atomistically. Whether used for apologetic or didactic purposes, background bits are likely presented without reference to a broader social, historical, or economic context. The ancient world is not understood in terms of its fundamental values and the interconnectedness of its institutions, what I will call its "contexture." A primary purpose of this chapter is to suggest ways to acquire a systemic understanding of a passage's contexture, and to that end we will identify helpful resources throughout.

The lack of contextual insight in our sermons may be explained by our ignorance, yet another factor is likely at work. Perhaps the *fear of not being relevant* keeps some of us from thoroughly exploring the Bible's ancient settings. With biblical illiteracy so widespread, we reason, people need to have a passage explained in simple terms that make sense in *our* world. Rather than allow our listeners to become aware of the gulf between us and the times of biblical writers, we want to build a bridge quickly to move the characters of the Bible into *our* surroundings. What might otherwise prove to be a disequilibrating encounter with an ancient writer becomes, instead, a familiar discussion of a domesticated text.

Cross-Cultural Encounter

The Bible's enduring, universal appeal should not be equated with cultural correspondence. Instead of immediate understanding, we should expect culture shock. Surely any law, poem, or historical account written 2,500 to 3,500 years ago should strike a modern reader as foreign. This is no less true for sacred Scripture. Reading the Bible is a sustained cross-cultural encounter. Distance and difference should be obvious; what is in common should be surprising. When preachers sensitively lead their listeners in this encounter, it will generate a wide range of effects. It can be fascinating, enlightening, enchanting, haunting, mystifying, and inspiring, all at the same time.

Hays and Duvall[2] have given us one of the best introductions to biblical interpretation. The authors describe the hermeneutical journey from "our town" to "their town" and back. The first interpretive act is to assess the width of the "river" that separates the two. Next we proceed to investigate the realities of their town. The trip back into our town requires constructing a "principalizing bridge" over which we carry salient principles with universal implications. The preacher who, for the sake of relevance, glibly locates a portion of Scripture in "our town" will, ironically, limit its capacity to challenge our world.

The investigation of the Bible's cultural context requires an attempt to reconstruct the "implicit knowledge" of its original listeners. This is a phrase Bible translators use as they consider the most effective way to render a passage into a new language. Without the aid of footnotes, translations often have to make explicit what the original writer left implicit. This notion is similar to "preunderstanding," a term used in hermeneutics. By this we refer not only to common knowledge, but also to the assumptions and perspectives shared by authors and their audiences. While reconstruction of these tacit realities is a tentative and provisional task, the only alternative is to leave implicit information to the imagination of contemporary readers. Films, for better and for worse, are quite determinative in filling in popular understandings of biblical accounts. Sometimes the biblical record (or a sermon) is challenged because it does not correspond to the movie!

The premise of this chapter is that any biblical passage should be understood first in terms of its original meaning in its original context. Only after this initial step does one determine appropriate implications for contemporary believers. This is in keeping with Walter Kaiser's frequent emphasis on the primacy (and accessibility) of authorial intention. We will now define cultural context and examine the tools we currently have to explore that context.

Layers of the Biblical World

Geographical and Historical Layers

The world of a biblical passage has many layers: geographical, historical, cultural, political, economic, and ideological. This multilayered milieu invites the use of a variety of social scientific disciplines: historical-geography, archaeology, history, anthropology, sociology, political science, and economics. Distinct yet interrelated dimensions of cultural systems reflect an intangible *Zeitgeist*, or "spirit of the times," which is important to appreciate.

Reconstruction of the biblical world begins with geography, studying what Monson[3] calls the "playing board." Understanding the playing board helps us to make sense of where people settle and travel, what they raise and trade, why they fight, and who they worship. We begin to understand the "rules of the game." The discipline of historical-geography has contributed to the identification of virtually all of the key sites mentioned in biblical accounts. With the help of a good Bible atlas the preacher can—and should—bear in mind the geographical setting of most Bible stories. There are now electronic atlases available through Logos and the Gramcord Institute.

Beyond site identification, historical geography has contributed to a growing awareness of regional characteristics. Because cultural systems, especially in pre-industrialized societies, are anchored to geographical realities, we can become familiar with the types of events and activities *characteristic* of each biblical region. For example, understanding the "open" character of Galilee and the "closed" character of Judea explains why some cities were taken by invading armies, why Phoenician Baal worship flourished where it did, and how Judea managed to be conservative religiously and politically. Understanding marginal rainfall patterns in the Judean Wilderness and Negev provides background for grain farming stories like Ruth and the mixed economy of a family like David's. The diversity in rainfall from North to South made centralizing worship around three harvest festivals a challenge. This puts into perspective

Jeroboam's rationale for moving the dates ahead a month for these festivals in the northern kingdom.

The classic work in this discipline is G. A. Smith's *Historical Geography of the Holy Land*, reprinted numerous times since it was authored in 1894. Monson's[4] work provides a compact up-to-date orientation to the playing board. A collection of related resources are published by Biblical Backgrounds.[5] Cleave's[6] atlases and CD-ROM provide the opportunity to view Israel's geography from above and to pull up high-resolution images of the major sites. Martin's[7] narrated helicopter tours over each region are extremely useful, and the six thousand slides in the Pictorial Lands of the Bible[8] collection offer excellent ground shots and many helpful notes.

Geography is more than simply the physical setting for war and work and worship. It is also a reservoir of images by which biblical authors described their aspirations, disappointments, counsel, and theology. The psalmist yearns for God in a dry and weary land, seeking spiritual refreshment like a deer panting for a water brook (Ps. 42:1). The sage finds wisdom by watching the ants and eagles (Prov. 30:19, 25). The judge knows that Yahweh expresses his pleasure and displeasure in the context of Israel's climatic realities (1 Sam. 12:17). The prophet anticipates a day when from the temple will flow a river that makes even the Dead Sea thrive with fish (Ezekiel 37).

Israel, the sacred space of God's activity, is the land of promise, a covenantal environment that serves in its own right as a primary theological category in the Old Testament. Preachers of our day need to recover this biblical orientation to understand how powerful the land was as a place of "gift, temptation, task, and threat."[9] The Promised Land anticipates our heavenly home, an object of hope in the New Testament.

Archaeological Layer

Historical geography makes it possible to reflect on the historical and theological significance of sites and regions mentioned in the Bible. This significance is understood with the help of a sister discipline, archaeology. By digging into "tells" (ancient settlements mounds) archaeologists uncover the "material culture" of previous occupation layers. Remains include artifacts that reflect the *realia* of daily life (cooking implements, tools, weapons, games) and structures that represent domestic and civil institutions (homes, city walls, temples, palaces).

Archaeologists are not merely interested in the finds that a given site yields. They are interested also in social and economic trends and political realities that are mapped onto the material culture. If Mycenaean pottery is found in Philistine sites in the Late Bronze Age, this confirms an Aegean origin for a larger migration of "Sea Peoples." When this pottery is found among Israelite settlements in the early Iron Age, it suggests trade with the Philistines. The influence of societies on each other is similarly evidenced in weaponry, architecture, and written documents.

Since the emergence of archaeology in the Levant (Syria-Palestine) in the early twentieth century, major shifts in the discipline have occurred. At first key sites were ravaged in search of spectacular finds. Jericho has been subjected to three major excavations partly to reconstruct the earliest archaeological activities. Over time more careful procedures were put in place including excavation in square grids between "balks." This makes it possible to document discoveries in the context of layers that are visible on the vertical surfaces.

One of the most important changes in archaeology is more philosophical than methodological. Increasing interest in everyday life now balances earlier concerns with historic geopolitical events. This reflects a commitment to a rounded social history. The larger personalities and their dramatic administrative and military actions are noted more often in official historical record. Archaeology seeks to reconstruct common or popular history by investigating, for example, ecological trends that explain settlement patterns.

Though now a remarkably complex discipline, archaeology is still as much art as science. The mute remains of the past require interpretation. We must also reckon with the fact that *most* of what we would like to discover no longer exists. Ancient sites were regularly demolished by invading armies, and the remains we do uncover are often quite random. The gaps in the record are unfortunately more impressive than the finds.

It would be helpful for any preacher to have a guide to archaeology and the Bible. Hoerth[10] has written a respectable evangelical resource. The standard in the field is by Mazar.[11] Comparison of these two makes it easy to see where conservative and mainstream scholarship differs. When using these resources it is useful to keep a chart of the archaeological periods in hand so the connections with biblical history are clear.

The Biblical Archaeology Society has a number of archaeology slide sets now available on CD-ROM. These are accompanied by detailed descriptions of each find. Images from this set provide useful background in a sermon where projection is available. A number of "Manners and Customs" books have been published over the years. These often refer to archaeological finds in order to explain the biblical world. Topical or chronological organization lends itself to appreciating specific phenomena in their larger historical-cultural context rather than exclusively in terms of a given Bible passage.

HISTORICAL LAYER

Historical geography and archaeology contribute to the discipline of history. Historians sift the results of these other disciplines (with a special interest in written sources) to reconstruct the ancient world. With the discoveries of hundreds of thousands of documents in the last two centuries, numerous points of contact between biblical passages and ancient Near Eastern (ANE) "parallels" can be discerned. Useful collections of relevant extrabiblical texts have been compiled by Pritchard,[12] Matthews and Benjamin,[13] and Hallo and Younger.[14] The tendency to deduce parallels became such a scholarly fashion that in 1961 S. Sandmel warned against the perils of superficial "parallelomania" in his Society of Biblical Literature presidential address.

While the process of reconstructing the history of Israel has inspired some extremes, there are numerous ways in which the effort has borne fruit. Walter C. Kaiser's *History of Israel*[15] is a readable introduction to biblical history that employs frequent reference to illuminating extrabiblical sources. For example, the date books of Thutmose III reflect an Egyptian template for recording battle accounts. Recognizing this model in Joshua helps us to date the book and to appreciate what it does and does not include. Other biblical stories have contemporaneous accounts written by their enemies. The "Moabite Stone" records how King Mesha viewed his struggle with the "house of Omri." Like Israel, the Moabites viewed victory and defeat as a result of the role of their patron deity. Mesha sacrificed his son to appease their god Chemosh. Hezekiah's survival during the attack of Judah in 701 BC is summarized by Neo-Assyrian King Sennacherib on the "Taylor Prism." While Sennacherib boasted over having Hezekiah "trapped like a bird in a cage," the prophet Isaiah explains how Yahweh delivered his royal city from this boasting threat (Isaiah 36–39). Parallel accounts bring us closer to the ground and make it possible to understand better how faith was expressed in practical terms.

Historians are not only interested in historicity—*that* certain events happened—but also in *how they were interpreted*. Parallels help us expose the orienting perspectives that are latent in historiographical sources. Biblical writers were not dispassionate, "objective" record keepers but theologians of history. In Jewish tradition the books from Joshua to Kings are called "The Former Prophets." This nicely captures the prophetic perspective of the writers. Long[16] does an effective job of looking at history as both fact (historical) and representation (historiographical).

Social History Layer

Unpacking the social history of ancient Israel requires the use of other social scientific disciplines. Anthropology is the comparative study of culture. The anthropological study of an ancient culture requires an acquaintance with geography and careful investigation of artifacts and sources. (Archaeology is a subdiscipline within anthropology.) As a comparative discipline, anthropology uses models from similar societies to develop types and taxonomies of social values and organizations. The study of Israel first as a tribal confederacy and then as an emerging monarchy has been the object of this kind of investigation.[17] The relationship of pastoralists to settled agrarian populations in the Near East has also been well researched. Ethno-archaeology is a subdiscipline that studies contemporary societies to understand ancient ones. This is possible among traditional cultures where types of behavior are perennial.

The anthropological lens clarifies patterns of family and village life that involve kinship, marriage, gender roles, trades, slaves and servants, hospitality, education, and mourning. It likewise provides insight into larger civic institutions associated with urban development and statehood. Urban realities include bureaucratic organization, public building projects, welfare systems, the integration of temple and religion into civic life, the role of prophets, and law codification. Some of these topics reach beyond anthropology to economics, sociology, political science, and law. Each of these fields has something to offer the student of Scripture.

The importance of these social sciences is their explanatory value. They help us make sense of a cultural matrix that might in turn explain surprises like Jephthah's vow (and his daughter's acquiescence), David's loyalty to Saul (even after his death), or the call for vengeance in the laments. Hofstede[18] explains that though culture has a physical, objective dimension to it (customs, behaviors, ceremonies, organizational structures), what *defines* a culture is a shared subjective dimension (perspectives, values, assumptions). He consequently defines culture as the "software of the mind." What holds together a given society is the common interpretation members attribute to their behaviors and buildings, their customs and conventions. This is their worldview.

Synthesizing the Data

Piecing together the objective and subjective dimensions of biblical cultures is not an exact science by any means. It requires synthesizing diverse data, considering reconstructed models, and exercising interpretive judgment. Balanced introductions to ancient Israelite life include those by Matthews and Benjamin,[19] King and Stager,[20] and Borowski.[21] The experimental journal *Semeia* has collected essays on *Old Testament Prophets* (1981) and *Honor and Shame* (1994). Other interesting insights have come from H. W. Robinson's *Corporate Personality in Ancient Israel*[22] and G. Anderson's *A Time to Mourn*.[23] My *Shepherds After My Own Heart*[24] explores the persistence of shepherd imagery in biblical discussions of leadership. These are samples of the kind of research that seeks out an indigenous rationale or inner logic to explain a major aspect of Israelite life.

Anthropological studies on Israelite religion have had a noticeable influence in Old Testament scholarship. M. Douglas[25] brought an anthropologist's perspective to Israelite law and E. Leach[26] explored the logic of Israelite sacrifice. Jewish scholar J. Milgrom[27] has provided an exhaustive commentary set on Leviticus that makes use of comparative studies. Notions of sacred space and time and the nature of Israel's priesthood (and prophets) have come under anthropological investigation. P. Miller[28] has a useful synthesis on a variety of cult topics. He also discusses the important distinction between popular and official religion in ancient Israel.

The Perspective of Presuppositions

As useful as these disciplines and resources are, they should be kept in perspective. Scholars employ conceptual models that betray the mental software of our own times. What might appear to be innocent "questions" and neutral "tools" are often the manifestations of academic guilds that have discernible presuppositional orientations. The preacher who wants to benefit from some of the resources mentioned needs an overview of the underlying issues.

First, one must reckon with an anti-supernatural bias. Many scholars insist that legitimate reconstructions of the past adhere to the constraints imposed by Enlightenment rationalism. In distinction from their "precritical" counterparts, modern historians are to assume a critical stance toward the sources and a disregard for supernatural elements.[29] Many archaeological and historical resources are attempts to explain Israelite history without recourse to a divine hand. From a similar vantage point, Old Testament parallels are frequently used as evidence against the claims of Israel's uniqueness. Israel is reduced to a mere symptom of pan–Near Eastern realities.

This skeptical orientation is at times useful. The believing community often uncritically accepts a traditional understanding of biblical texts. Our assumptions are also tainted by our own times. Interaction with alternative viewpoints can serve to highlight what a passage really does and does not affirm. For example, parallel creation accounts help underscore the strong monotheistic claims of Genesis 1. Numerous flood stories suggest widespread memory of a real event. Similarities in law codes highlight the egalitarian nature of the Mosaic law. J. Walton[30] has provided an excellent introduction to these kinds of comparisons.

There are other underlying trends in the social sciences. The *Annales* school, associated most often with F. Braudel, gives precedence to material culture over written documents in the reconstruction of past societies. This reflects a wider suspicion of ancient texts as ideologically charged propaganda that serve "official" state purposes. While this suspicion has extended to the study of the Bible as propaganda, the balance of interest in common history has been helpful. There is much more discussion now about the lives of the unnamed masses, the women, the socially marginalized. Domestic and village life is given its place alongside the urban centers of empire builders.

One element of the widespread critique of "modernity" is the recognition that scientific objectivity is an illusion. Criticism of the agendas of ancient authors has led to an awareness of contemporary agendas in historical scholarship. This awareness is not problematic for some. If the meaning is not in the text but is the result of our engagement with it, then we are encouraged to critique our sources from the perspectives of our diverse communities. Radical feminist criticism involves the application of a contemporary moral grid to ancient texts. Isolating the androcentric orientation of the authors is a primary goal. With its roots in Marxist economics, some expressions of liberation theology share this approach. Exegesis becomes an exercise in identifying the oppressive structures that a text betrays. This kind of scholarship begins by deconstructing the text and then uses it as a base for advocacy.

While evangelical preachers may prefer to avoid reading this kind of material, good insight is often mixed in with agenda-serving assertions and eccentric speculation. We only have two options: to become critical users of these resources (what K. Kitchen calls "spoiling the Egyptians") or to restrict our reading to those authors who share our convictions about the nature of Scripture. Unfortunately, while there are many evangelical scholars, the second approach would ignore the majority of scholarship in many disciplines. It would also insulate us from seeing things differently. We too are liable to domesticate the Bible and make it serve our agendas. The freedom with which the Bible's critics ask questions often makes it easier for them to challenge assumptions that have escaped our consideration.

Read Broadly

Reading broadly is also necessary for cultural competence in our own setting. Sometimes books of a more liberal persuasion are on the best-seller lists. Bruce Feiler's *Walking the Bible*[31] or Baruch Halpern's *David's Secret Demons*[32] quickly became authoritative sources about the Bible's characters and times and its historical value. Like films, these books are now a part of *our* cultural context and become the point of departure for discussing the portraits in Scripture. Reading them provides a chance to understand what our contemporaries find compelling—and gives us the opportunity to reassess traditional views.

The purpose of this chapter is to help pastors prepare for preaching the Old Testament. Most of what we have discussed to this point is a rationale for researching the cultural world and an orientation to the disciplines that provide resources. Now we turn to practical guidance for sermon preparation.

Preparing the Sermon

I recommend that preparation for preaching on a given passage begin with immersion. Read the passage in its larger literary context several times through to get an idea of the main thrust of it, its key ideas and images, and how it fits in the book. Then begin to align your preunderstanding with that of the ancient readers. Read about the historical period from a resource like Kaiser's *History*. If it is a story, follow it on an atlas map. Make a list of all of the background topics that might help explain the passage. For example, a list for Ruth 1 would include death, grief, kinship relations, interethnic marriage, domestic roles, famine, travel, Moabites, and village life in the early Iron Age. Making observations inductively is important before you open any commentaries. Look up these topics in Bible dictionaries, encyclopedias, or handbooks. You simply cannot expect commentaries to be thorough in their explanations of cultural background. Most have introductory sections that address author and setting, but you will want to become informed on a broad range of institutions, ideas, and images. *Zondervan's Illustrated Bible Backgrounds Commentary* and *The IVP Bible Background Commentary* series are designed to fill in this kind of background. The *IVP Reference CD* makes it possible to search topics throughout their *Bible Background Commentary: Old Testament, New Bible Dictionary, New Bible Atlas*, and *Dictionary of Biblical Imagery* (along with other New Testament resources). Searching by key word enables you to find relevant material outside the boundaries of a specific entry. Hallo and Younger[33] have published a three-volume collection of extrabiblical parallels that is now in searchable electronic (Libronix) form.

Another useful resource is the *United Bible Society's Handbook Series*, now available electronically in the Libronix environment. These guides serve missionary translators around the world. They unpack the "implicit information" behind each passage, explaining the cultural background that is taken for granted. Then they explore ways to create a "dynamic equivalence" translation. Using these guides is a great way to encourage thinking about our own culture as a target audience for whom clarity and understanding are crucial.

A systemic understanding of biblical cultures does not come simply through background study on specific passages. Occasionally one needs to read something general on biblical geography, archaeology, history, or anthropology. Consider a modest reading program that orients you to these fields.[34] You might subscribe to *Biblical Archaeology Review* or *Bible and Spade*. Become a periodic visitor at websites where chat sessions about archaeology and faith take place.[35] Finally, make a(nother) trip to the Holy Land. The sites and museums provide the best concentrated access to the contextures of Scripture.

Questions to Consider

1. What does it mean to read the Bible cross-culturally?
2. What are the ways the geographical, historical, archeological, and social history layers influence the preacher as he or she does research for a sermon?
3. How can one discern the theological perspective from which an author writes?
4. Reflect on how you can take the tips from this chapter and put them into practice in your sermon preparation.

On the Shelf

Hoerth, Alfred J., Gerald L. Mattingly, and Edwin M. Yamauchi, eds. *Peoples of the Old Testament World.* Grand Rapids: Baker, 1998.

Kaiser, Walter C., Jr. *Hard Sayings of the Old Testament.* Downers Grove, IL: InterVarsity, 1988.

———. *A History of Israel: From the Bronze Age through the Jewish Wars.* Nashville: Broadman & Holman, 1998.

Laniak, Timothy. *Shepherds After My Own Heart: Pastoral Traditions and Leadership in the Bible.* Leicester, UK: Inter-Varsity, 2006.

Walton, John H. *Ancient Israelite Literature in Its Cultural Context.* Grand Rapids: Zondervan, 1989.

9

Toward the Effective Preaching of New Testament Texts That Cite the Old Testament

Roy E. Ciampa

Preaching from passages in the New Testament that quote from or are otherwise based on or influenced by Old Testament texts poses special challenges and provides unique opportunities to the preacher committed to helping his or her listeners fully grasp the meaning and message of the preached text.[1]

The special challenges are related to the difficulties in understanding how an ancient author understood the relationship between an even more ancient biblical text and their own argument and the similarities and differences between the way ancient authors quoted and used texts and the ways we do today. Old Testament texts are not cited in the New Testament for their own sakes, but to meet the rhetorical needs of the

New Testament author. That is, New Testament authors do not provide disinterested commentaries on the meanings of Old Testament texts, but they cite those texts for a variety of reasons, primarily to make their argument clearer, more persuasive, or more authoritative. In order to effectively use a New Testament text that quotes the Old Testament, a preacher will want to help the embedded Old Testament text play the same role with their audience that it played with the original audience. For that to happen, a number of issues and misconceptions may need to be addressed.

The Variety of Uses of the Old Testament in the New

Most lay readers of the Bible tend to assume that New Testament authors always used the Old Testament as proof-texts to defend or support their theological arguments. Careful study of the issue, however, reveals that they quoted and alluded to Scripture for a number of reasons, of which defending or proving arguments was only one.[2] Among other possible functions of Scripture are those of clarifying by means of an illustration, revealing the significance of a contemporary event or reality, strengthening an author's credibility (by showing his abilities as an interpreter of Scripture),[3] or establishing a sense of rapport or communion with the readers.[4]

In each case the interpreter of the New Testament text where an Old Testament text is quoted should consider, but not prejudge, the purpose of the quotation. Is it intended to prove the author's point, or simply to illustrate or clarify it, or to serve some rhetorical purpose other than proof?[5] If an Old Testament text is referred to for illustrative purposes, it may be important for the preacher to clarify the illustration if the text is not a familiar one, since failure to do so may leave the author's point unclear. If the text is intended to support the argument of the New Testament author, it will be important to help the congregation understand how the Old Testament does that, since a failure to do so may make the author's point seem unfounded or illogical.

New Testament Authors as Biblical Exegetes and Biblical Theologians

When looking at the use of the Old Testament in the New, one of the key issues we often find ourselves facing is the way in which the authors of the New Testament developed and communicated their theology and their ethics. Many laypeople (and some pastors) treat the texts as though the biblical authors simply received their material through "divine downloads." That is, they imagine that divine inspiration entailed God's provision of new ideas and thoughts as a series of sudden "aha!" moments while they wrote their books.[6] Some people in our congregations probably suspect that the apostolic authors felt free to simply create new doctrines out of thin air, and almost as though by serendipity they were protected by God from saying or writing down things that were not true. Some scholars seem to think they simply chose from whatever ideas and concepts they happened to find in their environment, ideas and concepts that were attractive to them or seemed useful for the situation at hand. In some cases Paul is made out to be someone who creates his theological soup using a pharisaic concept as a base but spicing it up with a dash of stoicism and just a pinch of cynic philosophy. The evidence of Scripture (and a more robust doctrine of inspiration derived from it) suggests something different was going on.

Paul's exhortation to Timothy to "preach the word" and to "correct, rebuke and encourage—with great patience and careful instruction" (2 Tim. 4:2) comes right on the heels of his affirmation that "all Scripture is God-breathed and is useful for teaching, rebuking, correcting and training in righteousness" (2 Tim. 3:16). While Paul's words apply even to the New Testament, he was referring to what we call the Old Testament—the Bible of the early church. We should not find it surprising that Paul's letters and much of the rest of the New Testament often reflect a direct dependence on the Old Testament, as the books of the New Testament are dedicated to the tasks for which Paul understood the Scriptures to be useful.

It is significant that Luke tells us that the Bereans "were of more noble character than the Thessalonians, for they received the message with great eagerness and examined the Scriptures every day to see if what Paul said was true" (Acts 17:11). This is a remarkable statement since it implies that the Bereans, Paul, and Luke were all in agreement that the Bereans' attitude toward Paul and his message was not inappropriate but laudable! Paul's stance was not, "Oh, put your Bibles away, this is new revelation that God has given me and that you won't find there!" Rather, according to Luke's description, he evidently thought it appropriate and healthy for them to compare his message to the Scriptures. By his praise of the Bereans, Luke recommends that practice to his readers as well.[7] The authors of the New Testament clearly hold that the Old Testament is inspired by God and, as interpreted for them by the Lord Jesus Christ, it serves, along with the Lord's own teaching, as the ultimate authority for them and their churches.

While this chapter will focus on the preaching of New Testament texts that quote from the Old Testament, from the outset it needs to be said that the study and preaching of the New Testament should always entail a consideration of the way in which the message of the New Testament authors fits into and flows out of the pattern of revelation that had been previously communicated from God to his people. It is simply that special issues are raised for us when New Testament authors quote from or allude to specific texts and thereby clearly signal more specific contexts in which they expect their messages to be understood.[8]

Texts where biblical authors indicate to us how their views and arguments are based on Scripture serve as appeals to us and opportunities for us to grasp not just what they said but also how they theologized—how they came to that position and how the argument works. Wise preachers will take the opportunity to help their congregation move to a more profound understanding of arguments and of the theological underpinnings of the texts they read through a thoughtful retracing of the exegesis and theologizing of the biblical author.

The Old Testament as the Theological Context of the Writings of the New Testament

The New Testament is full of quotations from, allusions and references to, and echoes of the Old Testament. In these ways the authors of the New Testament reveal the theological and literary context within which their message is to be understood. For much of the history of the church, the books of the New Testament have been read primarily within the context of the rest of the New Testament (and later Christian theology), with the Old Testament playing a secondary role in its interpretation. When the books were originally written, of course, the readers were expected to understand them in the light of the Old Testament with the understanding that Jesus Christ (and the redemption he provides) was the ultimate and climactic fulfillment of the vision and promises of the Old Testament.

By helping a congregation grow in their understanding of the ways in which the arguments and theology of the New Testament are dependent upon an understanding of the Old Testament, a pastor or preacher may both demonstrate a personal love and passion for the Old Testament as the Bible of the authors of the New Testament and develop such a love and passion in the church that it becomes more "Berean" and less likely to fall into Marcionite ways of thinking.

Ancient Exegesis and Modern Prejudice

One of the problems for the modern exegete, and especially for the preacher, is that the ways the authors of the New Testament use the Old Testament seem so strange to most of us. Their quotations often do not match the texts as we read them in our Bibles and do not seem at first sight to have the meanings that the authors find in them. The bottom line is that the authors of the New Testament rarely quote and use the Old Testament the way we would if we were using the texts to support our own arguments. One of the issues that we need to face when addressing this subject is our tendency (and the tendency of every generation) to consider ourselves the ultimate standard for biblical interpretation against whose practices all others are to be found wanting. Each generation seems to think that their own approach to interpretation reflects the ultimate climax in hermeneutical advancement and that earlier interpreters are to be critiqued or vindicated in the light of contemporary norms. Such attitudes reflect an unfortunate kind of epistemological arrogance that fails to consider the possibility that moderns might have something to learn from interpreters of other times and cultures.

I am reminded of a famous scene from the film *Butch Cassidy and the Sundance Kid* where the two bandits are looking for legitimate work (ironically) as payroll guards. The Kid is asked to demonstrate his abilities as a marksman, but proves to be a dramatic failure. When asked to shoot a small object on the ground a stone's throw away, he misses it. He stands there, as expected, with his arm outstretched, staring carefully down the sights of his six-shooter as he slowly and deliberately squeezes the trigger. But he misses. As his would-be employer turns away in disgust, the Kid asks, "Can I move?" The boss doesn't understand, so the Kid demonstrates. In a flash he shifts sideways, draws his pistol from his holster, and, with two rapid shots from the hip, he shoots the object into the air and then immediately blasts the flying object into smithereens. Putting his pistol back in its holster he observes, "I'm better when I move." So he is a crack shot after all. He simply must be allowed to shoot his way rather than the way someone else might expect him to.[9] The biblical authors are also excellent (and divinely inspired) interpreters of Scripture. But they must be understood on their own terms (which were also the terms understood by their contemporaries) and not on the basis of whether or not they do things the way *we* might expect them to be done.

The biblical interpretation we find in the New Testament is often considered to be similar to our approach to interpretation, but lacking in one or two features that we expect to find. Among the features sometimes considered lacking is respect for the original literary and historical context of the quoted text. So biblical authors are often thought to provide us with "Interpretation Lite" (great intentions but less context).[10] The evidence suggests, however, that the ancient authors may be doing something *more* than we often do, and that those elements that we think reflect a lack of attention to the original context actually reflect the integration of other concerns that have informed the biblical authors' use of the Old Testament.[11] That is, a biblical author, studying our approach to interpreting the Old Testament, might conclude that *we* are the ones offering "Interpretation Lite" (great attention to a text in isolation but less integration with other relevant information). This reflects the fact that one of the things that tends to distinguish our post-enlightenment approach to interpretation is (at least until the more recent interest in cross-disciplinary integration) the great value that we tend to place on carrying out scientific investigations in carefully controlled and contamination-free environments. When it comes to biblical interpretation, that means we expect each passage to be interpreted on its own, in light of its grammar and syntax, the meanings of the individual words and the literary and historical contexts, and so on. We then expect each text to make its own individual and discrete contribution. In our ideal world, the meaning and applications of each text would also always be kept distinct. The New Testament authors reflect an acute awareness of the importance of grammar, context, and word meanings in their interpretations.[12] But they do not value compartmentalization and hermetically sealed working environments the way we do. So their interpretations of biblical texts often reflect insights and understanding that come from allowing their reading of any given text to be informed by any of a number of theological insights or relevant factors or pieces of information, and they do not usually separate out their exegesis and their interpretation, as we tend to do.[13]

The most obvious way in which ancient (and apostolic) interpreters would bring more (not less) than the context and meaning of a particular text into account in their interpretation is by bringing two or more texts together so that they might each shed interpretative light on the other (sometimes referred to by the rabbinic term *charaz*, "to string"). The most obvious texts to bring together were those that shared common terms or expressions. Later rabbinic literature uses the expression *gezerah shawah* for biblical interpretation that is based on interpreting two passages in light of each other because they share a term or expression.[14] When Jesus tells us that the two greatest commandments that summarize the law are Leviticus 19:18 ("love your neighbor as yourself") and Deuteronomy 6:5 ("Love the LORD your God with all your heart and with all your soul and with all your strength"), he is bringing together two texts that share the expression (literally) "and you shall love. . . ."[15] In Paul's discussion of justification in Romans 4, he brings together Genesis 15:6 ("Abram believed the LORD, and he credited it to him as righteousness") and Psalm 32:2 ("Blessed is the man whose sin the LORD does not count against him"). Both passages share the same term for crediting something to one's account.[16] In later rabbinic interpretation, the Bible is often treated like one enormous hypertext where any shared word invites a creative interpretation tying two or more texts together. In the earlier Jewish and New Testament uses of *gezerah shawah*, the ideas and passages that are brought together tend to share thematic (usually extending to the narrative plot and theological background and motifs of the passages) and not merely verbal ties, as in the cases cited here.[17]

Walter Kaiser has helpfully stressed the importance of discerning the role of "antecedent theology"[18] in the interpretation of texts. He points out that a biblical text cannot be "treated in abstraction and isolation from all that has *preceded* it in the history of revelation"; and he asks, "What is it that triggers appropriate association for the interpreter with biblical material on the same subject that has appeared *prior* to the time of this new addition to that same genre of revelation?"[19] We must seek to discern the "theology that 'informs' each Biblical text."[20] He points out "some of the clues to the antecedent theology in a text":

1. The use of the terms that by now have acquired a special use and taken on a technical status in the history of sal-

vation such as "seed," "servant," "rest," "kingdom," and "holy one";
2. A *direct quotation* of a portion or the entirety of an earlier word from God;
3. An *allusion* to a phrase, clause, sentence, or formula found in the earlier texts of Scripture;
4. An allusion or direct reference to earlier *events* in the history of Israel that had special significance for that day and all later generations of believers; and
5. A reference to the *contents* of God's numerous promises or covenants that formed the substance of His promise-plan for the created-redeemed order of the universe.[21]

Close attention to such clues to the antecedent theology informing any passage of Scripture is crucial to the implementation of Kaiser's important call for "a full involvement of Biblical theology as a part of our exegesis."[22] These also turn out to be some of the clues to the antecedent theology that may (alongside the original meaning and context of the citation itself) be informing not only the New Testament author's own text, but also his interpretation of a quotation within a given passage. Such antecedent theology must be carefully considered when deciphering the use of an Old Testament text in the New.

When preaching on a passage of the New Testament that quotes or alludes to a text from the Old Testament, the preacher may need to help the congregation understand what other texts or theological concepts or background is informing the author's understanding of and use of that text. These important parts of the background are not usually found on the surface of the text but depend upon a reader's (or listener's or preacher's) familiarity with the relevant background knowledge.

Some key parts of the hermeneutic assumptions informing that biblical theology include the following:[23]

- That due to corporate solidarity or representation, Christ, as the true king of Israel, represents his people and fulfills the role of true or ideal Israel. As in certain Old Testament passages, there may be a fluid relationship between statements regarding a representative figure and the people of God as a whole.[24]

- That God is working in history and unfolding his plan for the redemption of humanity and creation and that that plan entails the restoration of his original intentions for humanity and creation as indicated in the beginning of Genesis (with the image, glory, and righteousness of God reflected throughout all creation through God's divinely appointed human vice-regent[s]); and that this restoration is achieved through the redemption of Israel at the time of the exodus and the restoration of Israel and extension of salvation to the nations in another great act of redemption that will follow patterns established by the exodus (and is thus described as a "second exodus").
- That given God's sovereignty and consistency, there is and will be "a correspondence between what happened to God's people in the past and what happens now or in the future." Expectations for God's future actions are set by "climactic events in Israel's history," which also "become the paradigms by which new events are explained."[25]
- That the readers of the New Testament are living in the time of transition in which the age of eschatological fulfillment has begun and its consummation is to be awaited, and that Scripture was eschatological in its orientation, provided by God particularly (although not solely) for the instruction of God's eschatological community (the church)— especially for its understanding of Christ and the gospel.[26]
- That God's earlier revelations and promises are to be understood in light of his later and fuller revelation of his ultimate intentions.[27]

The Problem of Differing Texts

In many cases, when we (and those in our congregations) read the New Testament quotation of the Old Testament in our modern Bibles and then read the original Old Testament text in those same Bibles, they do not match. There are at least two different reasons for the differences. One reason is that the New Testament authors sometimes altered the text somewhat from the form in which they knew it. To understand this it helps if we realize that many of the criteria that we apply to the proper use of quotations today did not apply in the time of the New Testament. In our society, especially in legal contexts, quotations are expected to be absolutely precise and marked by quotation marks and with special indications of any omissions or alterations (such as ellipsis marks [. . .] or additional words placed in brackets). To alter the wording in any way without explicit indications of where the citation has strayed from the original is considered deceptive and unethical in our society. In the world of the New Testament, however, there were no such things as quotation marks[28] and people were free to exercise somewhat greater freedom in the way they quoted texts. The needs of the author and readers for clarity and relevance played a greater role in determining what was acceptable and what was not acceptable when quoting a text. Thus, if parts of the original text were deemed irrelevant to the argument of the person quoting it, they could be left out. Or, if changing a third person reference ("he" or "they") to a second person reference ("you") would put a sharper point on the quote and clarify its direct relevance to the readers, there was no reason not to introduce such an alteration.[29] If we can discern where a New Testament author has altered his text, highlighting some parts or ignoring others, it may provide an important clue regarding the particular relevance of that text to his argument.

Deciding just what alterations a New Testament author might have made to the quotation is also more complicated than most of our listeners are likely to assume, due to the second reason why some of the texts cited in the New Testament do not match what we read in our Bibles today. Comparison of the Masoretic Hebrew texts with those found in the Dead Sea Scrolls, the Samaritan Pentateuch, the Septuagint, and other ancient Greek and other versions (including the quotations found in the New Testament) suggests that the Old Testament was circulating in a variety of text forms in the time of the New Testament.

The authors of the New Testament often quote the Old Testament according to the text as it is translated in our modern Bibles, but where the quotation differs from what we find in our Bibles but agrees with a form of the text that is known to have been in use at the time, it may be helpful to explain to the congregation that the author was probably quoting the Bible according to the version (probably Greek) with which he was familiar and that it may also have been the version known to his readers. This practice of the biblical authors reflects a similar wisdom to that found in many modern preachers who prudently refrain from discussing every minor instance where they might disagree with the translation they are using, even if they have studied and read the original languages. They avoid correcting or criticizing the translation they are using (and that is likely to be used by the majority of the congregation) unless the translation issue happens to be essential to one of the main points they wish to communicate. Even imperfect translations (and, of course, they are all imperfect in one point or another) usually do an effective job of communicating the main points of a passage, and the same is true of the Greek versions of the Old Testament that were used by the authors and first readers of the New Testament. Whether the original author had read the text he is quoting in Hebrew or Aramaic or had only read it in Greek may be impossible for us to discern.[30] Even if he was aware of other translation possibilities, he may have considered it best to use the translation as it was known and read in the church(es) to which he was writing.

In many cases a preacher will not need to make any comments about the differences between the Old Testament text as found in our Bibles and the text quoted in the New Testament. In some cases, however, some explanation of the use and value of different Bible translations (both ancient and modern!) and the fact that they were used by the authors and readers of the New Testament will help the congregation understand both the value of the different translations they use or hear and the place of Bible translations in the early church. An explanation of the difference between fidelity to the exact wording of a text and fidelity to the meaning and point of a text and of the freedom enjoyed by New Testament authors to tailor their quotation for the sake of the clarity of their communication and application may go a long way toward helping the congregation understand a phenomenon that may seem strange to them.

The Importance of Both the Old Testament and the New Testament Contexts

Most modern readers will tend to assume that Old Testament quotations found in the New Testament were relevant for, and only for, the precise words that are used by the New Testament author. Although it is still highly debated,[31] many scholars now agree with C. H. Dodd in his argument that New Testament authors

> often quoted a single phrase or sentence not merely for its own sake, but as a pointer to a whole context—a practice by no means uncommon among contemporary Jewish teachers, as they are reported in the rabbinic literature. The reader is invited to study the context as a whole, and to reflect upon the "plot" there unfolded. In some way, an understanding of the plot will help him to see the significance of the strange events in the life and death of Jesus, and what followed.[32]

For example, the quotations from Isaiah 40:3 that we find in Matthew 3:3, Mark 1:3, and Luke 3:4 are not cited simply because John's message was taken from Isaiah, or because he fulfilled the text merely by preaching that message. The broader context of Isaiah 40 speaks of the good news that the exile (as a time of alienation not just from the Land, but also from God) would come to an end, and God's people would come to know his comfort, forgiveness, and presence. In the brief snippet of text quoted from Isaiah 40, the Gospel authors expect us to recognize an affirmation that the promised time of redemption was finally coming to fulfillment and that John was calling the people to prepare themselves to enter into it (or suffer the consequences of not preparing for that entrance). Of course, the words cited by the Gospel authors are particularly relevant to the author's point. It is not as though they would simply cite any bit of text within that chapter or section of the Old Testament book. The description of John "preaching in the wilderness" in Matthew 3:1 (immediately before the quotation), or "baptizing in the wilderness and proclaiming a baptism of repentance" in Mark 1:4 (immediately after the quotation), or that the word of God came to him "in the wilderness" in Luke 3:2 (two verses before the quotation) are simply ways of indicating that Isaiah's prophecy was being fulfilled by him.[33] The call to "prepare the way of the Lord; make his paths straight" is interpreted as a reference to John's call for repentance[34] as preparation for the coming of God's kingdom. As good preachers craft the wording of their own sermons with great care they will want to pay attention to the ways in which the biblical authors have carefully worded the text surrounding their Old Testament quotations in order to make their points unmistakable.[35]

The influence of the quoted text goes beyond the level of the precise words cited. It was indicated above that often the author intends to draw the reader's mind to the *context* of the words cited and not merely those precise words. In the context of Matthew's citation of Isaiah 40:3, we are told that John's message was that "the kingdom of heaven is at hand" (Matt. 3:2). In Isaiah 40 we are told that a herald will proclaim the good news of God's presence returning to his people and that the Lord "comes with power, and his arm rules for him" (40:10). In Isaiah 52:7 it is further clarified that the good news that would be proclaimed to Zion was that "your God reigns." Here, although John's words are not precisely the same as those found in Isaiah, the reader is expected to understand that John's message was an announcement that Isaiah's message of God's reign was unfolding before the eyes of his listeners. Just before Mark cites Isaiah 40 in his Gospel, he refers to "the gospel [good news] of Jesus Christ" (Mark 1:1), using the noun form of the Greek verb for "proclaiming good news" that is found in Isaiah 40:9.[36] The reader is to understand that the coming of Jesus Christ is the "good news" that Isaiah promised would be proclaimed to God's people in the time of salvation.[37]

Sometimes a text is quoted or alluded to in order that it might be interpreted. Other times it would be more accurate to say that the text is quoted in order that it might help the readers interpret something else (typically the situation in which the readers find themselves). Although no case falls completely into one category or the other, many of the Old Testament quotations in the New Testament primarily fit the second category,[38] and the quotations of Isaiah 40:3 fall mainly into the latter category. It is not so much that Matthew is interpreting Isaiah for his readers as that he hopes the reference to Isaiah will help his readers understand the meaning and significance of John's ministry. Of course, even in these situations an interpretation of the Old Testament text is assumed or implied. Where an understanding of the significance of the Old Testament text is assumed on the part of the author, the preacher will want to make sure his or her congregation understands what it is. In the case of the quotations from Isaiah 40:3, the congregation should understand the broader context and significance of Isaiah 40 as a call for Israel to prepare itself for the promised time of restoration when God would return to his people and deliver them. If the message of Isaiah 40 is to serve as a point of departure for understanding the significance of the Baptist's ministry and of the coming of Jesus Christ, it must be explained up front. But the stress should probably fall not on the interpretation of Isaiah, but on the interpretation of John (and Jesus) in light of Isaiah. Thus Matthew's point, for instance, is not found in the Old Testament text itself, but the Old Testament text serves as a hermeneutical key to understanding what had begun to take place in the time of John and had continued to his own day.

When interpreting or preaching on a New Testament text that quotes the Old Testament, one should consider the function of the Old Testament text in the broader New Testament context. It may play a role that goes far beyond the particular passage in which it is found. For example, Mark's quotations in the first three verses of his Gospel serve as a key to the theology and biblical interpretation of the Gospel as a whole. As Rikki Watts suggests, "Mark's introductory sentence (1:1–3) indicates his Gospel's conceptual framework."[39] Biblical quotes at or near the beginning of a book often play such key roles in orienting the readers' understanding of the theological stress of the work as a whole.[40] When preaching on such passages, one should carefully consider the role of the Old Testament quotation not simply within that particular passage but within the book as a whole. This would be especially important, of course, when preaching through such a book.

When biblical quotations and interpretation are encountered further on in a book of the New Testament, the exegete and preacher should discern whether or not there is prior biblical interpretation in that same book that is expected to inform the reading of the later text. For example, in Matthew's Gospel, the citation from Isaiah 40:3 (Matt. 3:3) is not found at the very beginning of the Gospel but comes after a significant amount of biblical context and biblical interpretation have already been provided. The quotation of that verse should not be interpreted in isolation but in light of Matthew's opening genealogy (which structures the history of Israel around the key turning points of Abraham, David, the exile, and then the coming of Christ, so that the coming of Christ is to be understood as the key to the ultimate end of Israel's exile and the final restoration promised by the prophets),[41] his quotation and interpretation of Isaiah 7:14 (and its evoking of the Immanuel theme of Isaiah), as well as the rest of the biblical interpretation that leads up to that verse.

By helping our congregations learn to understand the biblical interpretation found in the New Testament both in light of the context of the quotation or allusion in the Old Testament and in light of the broader context of the matrix of biblical interpretations found within the same book of the New Testament, preachers will help them avoid an atomizing approach to interpretation and will help them learn to understand such interpretation in terms of the larger theological plots and themes of both the Old Testament and the New Testament texts.

The Importance of Prior Biblical Interpretation

The Old Testament did not remain in a sealed room for centuries before being interpreted in the New Testament, and no New Testament author could expect to carry out his interpretation in a vacuum, as though no one had opinions about the meanings of passages before he wrote. In some cases New Testament authors oppose biblical interpretations familiar to their readers, in others they endorse them or presuppose them as common ground, and in others they qualify or nuance them. In some cases the interpretations with which they are interacting are made explicit (Matt. 5:21–48), in others we can only deduce what they were from an author's response to it (Gal. 2:14–21). Familiarity with the ancient interpretations of biblical themes and texts with which the biblical authors are interacting helps us make better sense of their arguments and interpretations. Good exegetical commentaries share that information, and effective preachers may need to share that information with their congregations to help them understand the arguments and positions of the biblical authors.[42] For example, Paul's discussion of Abraham and his justification (Gen. 15:6) must be understood in light of the way other Jewish teachers were interpreting the biblical material on Abraham.[43]

Conclusion

The issues related to understanding the use of the Old Testament in the New are many and complex. It requires wisdom to discern how much a congregation needs to know about these issues in order to reach a maximal understanding of the New Testament text without getting lost in the trees. In most cases the Old Testament quotation or allusion is not the point of the New Testament passage, but serves a supporting role, typically a very important one. A pastor is wise to remember to focus on the main point(s) of the text and to help the congregation understand how the Old Testament text illuminates and supports the New Testament text without allowing the sermon to become a lecture on ancient biblical interpretations or arguments.

Here are a few questions a preacher needs to ask of a text that includes a quotation from the Old Testament:[44] What was the original context of the Old Testament text? Does the New Testament use reflect the influence of the Old Testament context? Has the Old Testament text been interpreted in later parts of the Old Testament or in other early Jewish or New Testament texts? Does the New Testament use reflect familiarity with those earlier interpretations? What other Old Testament texts are cited, alluded to, echoed, or otherwise inform this New Testament passage? Does the New Testament citation reflect one of the textual forms known to us from the period (the Masoretic text, the Septuagint, the Dead Sea Scrolls)? Has the New Testament author modified the text in any way? If so, does that modification of the text affect its meaning or simply help the readers see the relevance of the text for their situation? How does the Old Testament text function in the context of the New Testament author's argument or narrative? How much of this information does my congregation need to know in order for the Old Testament text to function for them the way it did for the original readers of this passage?

Questions to Consider

1. What are some of the reasons New Testament authors quoted from the Old Testament?
2. What role does theology play in the quotation of Old Testament texts in the New Testament?
3. Discuss the function of context when Old Testament texts are quoted by New Testament authors.
4. Reflect on how you can take the tips from this chapter and put them into practice in your sermon preparation. What's your plan?

On the Shelf

Beale, G. K., ed. *The Right Doctrine from the Wrong Texts? Essays on the Use of the Old Testament in the New.* Grand Rapids: Baker, 1994.

Carson, D. A., and G. K. Beale, eds. *Commentary on the Use of the Old Testament in the New.* Grand Rapids: Baker, forthcoming.

Dodd, C. H. *According to the Scriptures: The Sub-structure of New Testament Theology.* London: Fontana, 1952.

Ellis, E. Earle. *The Old Testament in Early Christianity.* Tübingen: J. C. B. Mohr Siebeck, 1991. Reprint, Grand Rapids: Baker, 1992.

Hays, Richard B. *Echoes of Scripture in the Letters of Paul.* New Haven and London: Yale University Press, 1989.

Kaiser, Walter C., Jr. *The Uses of the Old Testament in the New.* Chicago: Moody, 1985.

Longenecker, Richard N. *Biblical Exegesis in the Apostolic Period.* Grand Rapids: Eerdmans, 1999.

10

Preaching the Old Testament Today

David L. Larsen

The Premises for Preaching the Old Testament

The sheer bulk of the inspired Old Testament Canon demands our measured attention to this three-quarters of our Scripture (which is the referent of 2 Tim. 3:16–17). The apostle Paul did not hesitate to "proclaim . . . the whole will of God" (Acts 20:27). The Old Testament was the Bible of our Savior, the apostles, and the early church. We cannot understand them or their work if we ignore the fount from which they drank or the authoritative library from which they read. There are also the special *afficionados* of the Old Testament in every congregation who glow with joy when it is expounded. They always hearten and encourage us.

Of course, the center of gravity for believers is the New Testament in its magnificent presentation and portraiture of Christ, our divine Savior and Lord, and in the apostolic witness to his total all-sufficiency. We are sorely tempted to bed down in these later documents and luxuriate in their succulent provision. In this we would be abetted by those modern-day Marcionites (some of whom are in every local assembly) who share with their ancient namesake an awkward aversion to the older Testament and so express themselves to their pastor-teachers. Often they are apologetic for their distaste, but it is real and painful.

If only in the interest of variety and balance in our preaching (not inconsequential considerations), we need to review the percentage of our use of Old Testament texts. If one-third of our preaching is from the fabulous richness of the Old Testament we are above the average, but less than one-fourth would seem to be pathological. Ten percent or less is abysmally low. Such minimalism demands address.

The premises for reasserting the relevance of preaching the Old Testament need to be revisited by every practitioner of the craft on a regular basis. In this concern I would like to offer some considerations "toward" the case (to use a familiar Kaiserian modesty) for preaching the Old Testament.[1]

We Need to Preach the Old Testament because It Lays the Foundation for All That Follows

Whether it is a family with its roots, a building and its foundation, or any historical event—what precedes and comes before are of immense significance. The modern disdain for history deprives us of connectedness and leaves us in a cut-flower isolation. We need our Old Testament.

1. The Genesis account of the creation of all things by God is the prolegomena to all reality. The creator/creature distinction is vital to our worship and the safeguard against idolatry. Human worth is predicated on our being created in God's image, and the nature of marriage is defined in terms of the Genesis account of God making of Adam and Eve one flesh (Matt. 19:4–6). A constant theme of worship in both Testaments is the focus on the God who created all things (Rev. 4:11).

2. How could we meaningfully preach the depravity of the human race without Genesis 3 and the narrative of a historic fall? Seeing humankind in Adam or in Christ has a frame of reference in Genesis 3. Any probing analysis of our predicament in sin drives us back to the primal rebellion. How innocence was lost sets up the Genesis/Revelation comparison and contrast between our first parents in a beautiful garden and the ultimate recovery of redemption in the garden of the city of God (Revelation 20–22).

3. With such a large investment of the Old Testament in the beginnings and history of God's ancient covenant people, Israel, without giving full attention to this holy history we would be sundered from the context in which Christ and the early church lived and ministered. Geopolitical Israel is mentioned forty-five times in the New Testament, and Paul's argument in Romans 9–11 would be incomprehensible without the Old Testament narrative. Christianity is vitally a historical religion, but if sundered from its history, it is cast loose as an orphan bereft of its forebears. In my view, the church does not replace Israel but the analogues of replacement theology are critical. Believers today are the spiritual sons and daughters of Abraham (Gal. 3:7). How can we preach the new covenant of Hebrews without Jeremiah 31? How can we enter into the Lord's Supper without the background of Passover? How wretchedly impoverished we would be without the whole Bible, and without the Old Testament, the New Testament people of God would be shorn of our roots.

4. The absolutely crucial New Testament teaching about a blood-mediated salvation has its foundation carefully laid in the Old Testament sacrificial system and in the peculiar nature of blood atonement. The altars with the sacrifice of innocent life for the guilty are the indispensable preface to the New Testament teaching about a substitutionary atonement, and Isaiah 53 affords us a preview of Christ's dying love on Calvary. Scripture nowhere countenances a gnostic extrication of Christ from a truly human and earthly existence (yet without sin)—the Son of God was a Jew of the first century and profoundly a part of an earthly people with a history and a suffering and a hope. Efforts to sanitize the Savior from whence he came have been

disastrous to the faith through the ages up to Adolf Hitler and others in our own time. How can a Christian be an anti-Semite? The Old Testament is bone of our bone and flesh of our flesh.

5. Apocalyptic writing in the New Testament (whether in the Olivet Discourse, 2 Thessalonians 2, Jude, or the Revelation) has its DNA in Isaiah, Daniel, and Zechariah. The unity of Scripture is no surprise to us considering the divine authorship of the whole revelation (2 Peter 1:19–21). Whether we are dealing with the cunning of Satan, the personalities of the end-time, the period of great distress for the people of God (the messianic woes), or the ultimate triumph of the kingdom of God, we sense in this impressive tapestry more than a thematic unity—there is an organic unity that leaves us with a complex but coherent scenario in which "the God of heaven set[s] up a kingdom that will never be destroyed, nor will it be left to another people" (Dan. 2:44). The foundation blocks for everything in the New Testament are laid in the Old Testament, and "when the foundations are destroyed, what can the righteous do?" (Ps. 11:3).

We Need to Preach the Old Testament because It Is the Inspired Anticipation of Jesus Christ the Messiah

Since the apostolic witness was so Christ centered and since the great apostle Paul resolved "to preach Christ and him crucified" (1 Cor. 2:2), today's preachers understandably feel remiss in doing otherwise. We have often been reminded of the young preacher who found the plea in his pulpit one Sunday: "Sir, we would see Jesus." He then preached Christ with abandon and found the next Sunday the response: "Then were the disciples glad when they saw the Lord." So where does this leave us with regard to the Old Testament?

Not only does the Old Testament contain building blocks which form the structural footings of our grand doctrines and theology, but suffusing and permeating the whole is the person and presence of the Savior. Thus indeed the gospel was announced in advance to Abraham (Gal. 3:8). Jesus clearly affirmed that the Scriptures "testify about me" (John 5:39) and to the two disciples on the road to Emmaus "beginning with Moses and all the prophets, he explained to them what was said in all the Scriptures concerning himself" (Luke 24:27).

In what sense is Christ everywhere in the Old Testament? This has been much discussed. Some have argued that inasmuch as human fallenness and sin are everywhere on the pages of the Old Testament, we have in fact Christ present on each such page, since he is the only redeemer and Savior from sin. While this is true, the argument really dodges the actual question concerning in what respect the Christ pervades the Old Testament.

Walter Kaiser has consistently focused on the promise/fulfillment motif in Old Testament theology. From the protoevangelium of Genesis 3:15, the Old Testament pulsates with the promise of redemption to be fulfilled in and through the person and work of Jesus Christ. The preacher-exegete must at all times demonstrate "exegetical integrity" (2 Tim. 2:15). Kaiser has been unyielding in his insistence on seeking the author's intention in a text and in seeking the single meaning of the text. In an age of reader-response and literary deconstruction (in which many postmoderns will deny that there is any text), Kaiser has always held the high ground—what does the text actually say?

Given the progressive nature of divine revelation, we must beware of bringing subsequent disclosure into a specific Old Testament passage. How then shall we speak of Christ as being present in the Old Testament?

1. The Old Testament abounds with several hundreds of predictive prophecies concerning the Messiah. Holy Scripture is absolutely unique in its possession of such a body of predictive prophecy. This is because God knows all things and has been pleased to make many of these coming realities known through his Word. His ability to foretell the future sets the true and living God apart from idols (Isa. 44:8; 45:21; 46:9–10). In the synagogues almost five hundred Old Testament passages were denominated messianic. These are a treasure trove for the New Testament preacher.

The New Testament stress on the fulfillment of Old Testament prophecy is clearly built on the presupposition of its actual existence. That Christ was to be born of a woman, as the seed of Abraham through Isaac and of the fourth son of Jacob is clear. That the Messiah would be a prophet like Moses and a sin-bearer for the race and that he would suffer and die as the means of propitiation are right there. Where he would be born, his earthly poverty, the precise circumstances of his death, and the certainty of his resurrection from the dead are all laid out in meticulous detail. This is biblical supernaturalism and is as objectionable to liberal critics as the complementary idea that the essential scenario of the wrap-up of human history is laid out in numerous prophecies about the end-time.

2. The Old Testament is also replete with types or correspondences between earlier and later persons and events. Although types have been sadly abused (as when one commentator insisted that Abraham's servant in quest of a bride for Isaac depicts forty aspects of the Holy Spirit's creation of the church as the bride of Christ), the New Testament explicitly says of Israel's journey from Egypt, "that rock was Christ" (1 Cor. 10:4). This is the basic hermeneutic of the book of Hebrews. There can be no doubt about the brazen serpent lifted up in the wilderness, the manna, Passover, Jonah in the fish, or Hosea's marriage. These are explicit in the New Testament. Great caution should be used with what appear to be implicit types—such as the cities of refuge, the life of Joseph, the Jewish Sabbath and religious calendar—but they have validity. The Tabernacle in the wilderness sets forth great truths with regard to a sinner's approach to a holy God but considerable caution should be used in making every pin and thread a type of Christ.

3. The Old Testament sets forth the long and extraordinary process of preparing the way for the coming of the Messiah. If the Old Testament is Act One of the drama and the New Testament is Act Two, we could hardly preach Act One without some testimony or reference to the fact that Act Two (its fulfillment) has now taken place. To preach an Old Testament text as a Rabbi would preach it would in fact be a betrayal of the gospel. We must not hint or imply more in the text than is there, but

Christ the Messiah is the frame for the picture of redemption. The theme of the Bible is salvation and deliverance—the older Testament looks forward to it in the Christ-event and the newer Testament looks back upon the actualization of the promises in our Lord Jesus Christ.

How conceivably could a preacher of evangelical faith give short shrift to any part of the Scriptures which Christ and his apostles loved and venerated? These are "the holy Scriptures which are able to make us wise for salvation through faith in Jesus Christ" (2 Tim. 3:15). The apostle Paul intoned his confidence that "everything that was written in the past was written to teach us, so that through endurance and the encouragement of the Scriptures we might have hope" (Rom. 15:4). As Philip "began with that very passage of Scripture [Isaiah 53] and told him the good news about Jesus" (Acts 8:35), so every servant of the Word has the high privilege of handling the whole Bible—including our precious Old Testament with its incomparably rich veins of spiritual ore which both magnify and glorify our Lord Jesus Christ. The message must be shared.

We Need to Preach the Old Testament because It So Poignantly Provides a Rich Pictorialization of God's Plan of Eternal Redemption and Its Implications

Paul the apostle saw the experiences of the children of Israel on their journey toward Canaan as *examples, figures, copies, images* (1 Cor. 10:6), and this "to keep us from setting our hearts on evil things as they did." He goes on to say, "These things happened to them as *examples* (or *copies*) and were written down as warnings for us, on whom the fulfillment of the ages has come" (10:11).

The visualization and imaging of revealed truth have always been important in its communication. Our Lord's use of parables makes that quite plain. But we live in an incomparably visual society in which images seem to matter much more than ideas (although in fact images are not possible without a modicum of ideas). Nonvocal is really a better way to speak of such than nonverbal. A picture is better than a thousand words is an old saw, although it reflects the contemporary disparagement of the verbal quite characteristic of the preference for the noncognitive.

The homiletics of the left has gone for narrative to the virtual exclusion of all other literary genres. The result has been narrative theology, narrative ethics, narrative spirituality, and so on. The present fixation on narrative (which is ultimately faddish, in my judgment) nevertheless does point out the invaluable treasure we possess in biblical narrative, recognizing that almost half of our Bible is narrative.[2] Conservatives have always loved the narrative sections, but we have tended to lose the power of the story line by using too traditional a rational grid imposed on the story. The oceans of books on narratology have summoned us to a new and more thoughtful analysis about how we might better use the resources we have in biblical narrative and what they might mean for our time. The biblical use of narrative is deliberate and is an open door to increased and more effective utilization of this intriguing biblical genre.

At the same time we must beware of a serious pitfall. With all of its communicative attractiveness, narrative has a serious limitation not always observed. Doctrine cannot be built on narrative since by its incidental nature, it is one happening and therefore incapable of generalization. Liberals sought to build soteriology on the parable of the prodigal son (Luke 15). Their construct required no cross or atonement. The parable does not contain any expiation. Similarly, the liberal establishment found a soteriological jewel in the sheep and goats judgment of Matthew 25:31–46. Acceptance in the adjudicatory hinges on good deeds and benevolence and boils down to a raw Pelagianism. Needless to say, the cross of Christ is again extraneous. The narratives of our Lord's crucifixion are profoundly moving but do not themselves yield a doctrine of the atonement, that is, they do not set forth why it is that Christ must die and how that relates to our sins. We need the didactic sections of Scripture to explain to us that "Christ died for [*huper*] the ungodly" (Rom. 5:6) and that "God made him who had no sin to be sin for us, so that we might become the righteousness of God" (2 Cor. 5:21). In other words, the mighty acts of God need an authoritative interpretation. What does the story mean? Sometimes the interpretation is right there or in the context as in some parables of Jesus. As every preacher knows, an illustration is an irreplaceable clarification of a point asserted or the further emotional charging of that point.

What better way to show how "faith comes by hearing the message" (Rom. 10:17) than by tracing the growth of faith often in fiery testing in the life and experience of Abraham, the father of all who believe? The dialectic of values—sacred and profane—becomes so vivid and real in the lives of Jacob and Esau. First suffering and then glory is adumbrated in the experience of Joseph. These powerful narratives although chronicling events of four millennia ago have an existential immediacy that is gripping and convincing.

To avoid the vapid moralizing into which we preachers so easily slide, we need the bracing doctrinal axioms from the lips of our Lord or the pen of the apostles. Of course we must be exceedingly wary of strong-arming a theology on a narrative such as the esteemed brother who wanted to illustrate the five points of Calvinism out of the story of Mephibosheth at King David's table (2 Samuel 9). Now depravity may be in the narrative in the crippling of both feet, but where is limited atonement?

How better to be convincing on the principles of divine providence as stated in the Psalms or the Epistles than to consider the amazing little book of Ruth which sage Samuel Johnson called the most perfect short story. But it is more than a story—it shows how God developed the messianic line and provided for a young woman who embarked upon the pathway of faith out of Gentile darkness. This must be the authorial intention of relating Eliezer's quest for a bride for Isaac (Genesis 24). The cruel fate of the Jews before the arch anti-Semite Haman exposes the gracious strategy of the divine providence in sparing and using his people in Esther. Paul's passion to go to Rome and the delays he encountered unlock many insights as to how the Lord guides and directs his servants (see Romans 1, 15). Spiritual warfare (Ephesians 6) is well seen on the pages of the David cycle and in the experience of Gideon the hesitant hero. The difficult doctrine of sanctification comes alive out of Romans 6 in Old Testament narrative. It is interesting that Paul himself senses the need for some personalization as he shares with us in Romans 7. The anecdotal does not establish doctrinal principle but does illustrate and illuminate it.

The most neglected of any literary genre in either Testament is the prophetic and apocalyptic. Although its imagery is unique, apocalyptic is a kind of narrative—it is linear and dramatic. Mounting biblical illiteracy has altered the frequency and nature of our use of biblical illustration, but biblical narrative still represents an ocean of help and power in our use of the teaching sermon, which is really what biblical exposition is: "Preach the Word!" (see 2 Tim. 2:2).

We need to preach the Old Testament as it assists us in the complex task of application

One of the most arduous responsibilities of the biblical preacher is to make careful application of the text, moving it from then to now. Some of the homileticians of the left with a deficient view of biblical authority have felt that application is patronizing and condescending, but the expositor sees ample biblical precedent for showing how the meaning of the text has contemporary significance (Neh. 8:8; Luke 4:21; 2 Tim. 3:16–17).

The Ten Commandments are in fact the ramifications of who God is—"I am the LORD your God"—and what he has done—"who brought you out of the land of Egypt, out of the land of slavery" (Exod. 20:2). This is the invariable pattern in Scripture—the doctrinal fact and reality from which then necessarily follow standards of conduct. Creed moves to conduct and belief requires behavior, and this is the pattern in Romans, Ephesians, Colossians, and elsewhere. Some have argued that there is more heresy in application than in any other aspect of preaching. The necessary safeguard against heresy or moralism is to build application carefully from the basic theology of the text.

The moral law of the Old Testament is theological. Ethics in the older Testament (and in the later Testament as well) is inferential from the nature and character of God. The law is "holy, righteous and good" (Rom. 7:12) because it is derived from who God is. The law was never intended to be the instrument for the salvation of sinners (Acts 13:39; Rom. 3:20). But the law must be used "properly" (1 Tim. 1:8); in other words, "the law was put in charge to lead us to Christ" (Gal. 3:24). In coming to Christ, the justified believer does not change gears for the living of the Christian life, as though "after beginning with the Spirit" we now try to attain our goal "by human effort" (Gal. 3:3). Rather, "the righteous requirements of the law are fully met in us, who do not live according to the sinful nature but according to the Spirit" (Rom. 8:4).

"The righteous requirements of the law" stand, and Kaiser's substantive work in Old Testament ethics assists in our understanding of how monogamous marriage, sexual chastity, and high standards for family life follow from the unique revelation of who God is. Respect for life, generosity to strangers and foreigners, and personal holiness are to be the trademark of God's people because God is holy (Lev. 19:2; 20:7, 26; 21:8). How we treat our neighbors and the destitute is explored with care. How we handle wealth and possessions is addressed. The standards of truth and justice are definitively dealt with. Differing here from the Theonomists and Dominion theologians who see the call of the church to be the reestablishment of the theocracy upon earth in this age, we would see this invaluable disclosure of the divine will as a model for the application of revealed truth, especially as this unique trove is reaffirmed in the New Testament (with the exception of the Sabbath laws). What the Old Testament says about homosexuality and abortion is most germane.

Another rich resource for help in application is the wisdom literature of the Old Testament. The Psalter is not only our historic first book of worship and praise, but we observe the application of divine truth particularly in the seventy-three psalms that bear the David-title in his triumphs and trials, in his moral debacle, and in his family strains. The book of Proverbs furnishes us with limitless insights into the life that is lived by "the wisdom that is from above" (James 3:13–18). Here we learn about filial piety, caution in the use of alcohol, civic duty, and interpersonal relationships. The folly of laziness, the danger of falsifying the truth, and the advantages of generosity are vividly set before us.

The process of application, then, properly involves the careful and nuanced identification of the principle of scriptural truth to be applied, intertextual exploration of relevant parallels (*analogia scripturae*) including the wonders of the Old Testament, and then the placement of the principle clearly in a contemporary context through current reference, anecdote, or appeal.

In sum, we have attempted to show at least four major respects in which our exquisitely beautiful and precious Old Testament is a necessary source of much preaching by expositors of our time. The more the New Testament means to us, the more the Old Testament will mean to us.

Ad Gloriam Dei.

Questions to Consider

1. How does the Old Testament form the foundation for all that follows?
2. How does the Old Testament function in terms of anticipating the Messiah?
3. With what issues must preachers grapple as they work with narrative literature?
4. What are some of the challenges you face in your preaching context as you try to apply Old Testament texts?
5. Reflect on how you can take the tips from this chapter and put them into practice in your sermon preparation. What's your plan?

On the Shelf

Chapell, Bryan. *Christ-Centered Preaching*. Grand Rapids: Baker, 1994, 2005.

Clowney, Edmund P. *Preaching Christ in All of Scripture*. Wheaton: Crossway, 2003.

Greidanus, Sidney. *Preaching Christ from the Old Testament*. Grand Rapids: Eerdmans, 1999.

Kaiser, Walter C., Jr. *The Messiah in the Old Testament*. Grand Rapids: Zondervan, 1995.

———. *Toward Old Testament Ethics*. Grand Rapids: Zondervan, 1983.

Preaching the Old Testament Evangelistically

Robert E. Coleman

No one in the academy has given more distinction to the subject of this chapter than Walter C. Kaiser Jr. Not only that, he stands tall in the best tradition of higher education in America, as expressed by the founders of Harvard College in 1641: "Everyone shall consider the main end of his life and studies is to know God and Jesus Christ, which is eternal life."[1]

It is understood, of course, that bringing people to know Christ involves more than making converts. The Great Commission stipulates that we are to "make disciples," meaning learners who follow Jesus (Matt. 28:19–20).[2] Evangelism is the proclamation of Christ, Savior and Lord, but as the Lausanne Covenant states, "In issuing the Gospel invitation we have no liberty to conceal the cost of discipleship."[3]

What then makes a sermon uniquely evangelistic? To be sure, all Christian preaching should some way lift up the name of Jesus, the name above every name, whether the sermon be a declaration of the facts of personal redemption or the teaching of some great moral truth. But in a more specialized sense, evangelistic preaching concerns the message of salvation, a message that carries with it the expectation of a response to the claims of Christ in true faith and obedience. Such preaching does not necessarily require any particular type of sermon or homiletical method; rather it involves preaching distinguished by the call for commitment to the Son of God, who died for our sin and rose victorious from the grave.[4]

Christ-Focused

I suggest three principles to keep in mind when preparing to preach evangelistically. These criteria are by no means exhaustive, but they offer some basic guidelines.

The place to begin is with Jesus. To make a sermon without Christ would be like trying to make bread rise without yeast. Charles Spurgeon was right on when he told his students: "Preach Christ, always and everywhere. He is the whole gospel."[5] The Bible comes alive in Jesus. He is the Word made flesh. Summing up this all-encompassing theme of Scripture, the apostle John said, "These are written that you may believe that Jesus is the Christ, the Son of God, and that believing you may have life in his name" (20:31).

Lest one imagines that his statement applies just to the New Testament, recall that it was only the Old Testament that existed when Jesus said, "These are the Scriptures that testify about me" (John 5:39). Clearly he accepted the Bible of his day as a witness to himself (Luke 4:16–21; cf. Isa. 61:1–2).

Take as an example the account of Jesus speaking with two disciples on the road to Emmaus following the resurrection. "Beginning with Moses and all the Prophets, he explained to them what was said in all the Scriptures concerning himself" (Luke 24:27; cf. Deut. 18:15; Isa. 7:14; 9:6; 40:10–11; 53:1–12). "After breaking bread with them he said, 'Everything must be fulfilled that is written about me in the law of Moses, the Prophets and the Psalms.' Then he opened their minds so they could understand the Scriptures. He told them, 'This is what is written: The Christ will suffer and rise from the dead the third day, and repentance and forgiveness of sins will be preached in his name to all nations'" (Luke 24:46–47).

The apostles learned from their Lord to preach the Old Testament the same way (Acts 2:14–34; 3:11–26; 8:35; 13:23–35; 17:2–11; 1 Cor. 15:3–4). They saw in Christ the fulfillment of all that had been written. The full sweep of redemptive history was focused in the person, work, and teaching of the Savior (Matt. 1:23; Mark 1:1–3; Luke 1:1–3:37; John 1:1–18).[6]

With Christ at the center, the two Testaments are brought together in a beautiful unifying witness to the gospel of grace. Not that the Old Testament is totally about the Messiah, for the "God-breathed" sacred writings speak to many needs and "are useful for teaching, rebuking, correcting, and training in righteousness so that the man of God may be thoroughly equipped for every good work" (2 Tim. 3:16). Much of this equipping purpose of Scripture, of course, relates to evangelism by developing the Great Commission ministry of disciples. But supremely, an evangelistic approach to the Bible looks for ways to make one "wise for salvation through faith in Christ Jesus" (2 Tim. 3:15).

Sidney Greidanus in his book *Preaching Christ from the Old Testament*, very ably points out seven ways that a Christocentric interpretation may take form.[7] One method is to see a passage of Scripture in the historical progression of God's redemptive plan through history, beginning in creation, moving through Israel, leading to Christ, then the church, and finally consummating in the new creation. Another approach proceeds by way of promise fulfillment, seen first in Genesis 3:15, moving to Abraham (Gen. 12:1–3), into David (2 Sam. 7:16), proliferated with messianic promises.[8]

Typology offers another method, moving from a type in an Old Testament passage to the anti-type in Christ. Or one can go the way of analogy, showing the relationship between God's message for Israel and Christ's message to the church. The longitudinal method traces a theme of the Old Testament to Christ in the New Testament. A different approach can take a

New Testament quote, which cites or alludes to an Old Testament passage linking it to Christ. A final way is to show the contrast that Jesus has brought to an Old Testament passage. The idea is to select the method that brings out the most compelling witness.

As an example, the theme of the blood could be developed by almost any of these approaches. The term is used 460 times in the Bible, 362 of them in the Old Testament.[9] When related concepts are included, such as altar, sacrifice, offering, covenant, atonement, redemption, and many others, the blood presents endless ways to bring one to the cross of Christ.

I recall hearing a missionary tell about a boy who appeared at a mission hospital in Kenya with a gaping wound in his foot. He had been accidentally injured while cutting grass with a friend in the jungle. Part of his heel was cut off. Without waiting to inform anyone of the mishap, the two boys set out across country to find the mission station where they knew help was available. Every time the little foot touched the sandy earth, it left a faint trace of blood. The journey was long and difficult, but at last they arrived.

After a time the boy's mother appeared. The doctors were surprised that she found the way. There were no well-defined trails, and she had never made the trip before.

"How did you do it?" she was asked. The dear woman, overjoyed to be with her child, replied, "Oh, it was easy. I just followed the blood."

In a much more profound sense, that is how we come to Jesus. The path is sometimes rough and may lead through many trials, but we need not fear getting lost. All we have to do is follow his footprints. They are easy to find, for each one is stained with blood. Whether in the Old Testament or the New, the blood will lead to the Savior.[10]

However developed, an evangelistic sermon lifts up Christ. He is the Evangel, "the Good News" incarnate, "the Lamb of God who takes away the sin of the world" (John 1:29; cf. Gen. 22:8; Isa. 53:7). In him every redemptive truth begins and ends. "There is no other name under heaven given to men by which we must be saved" (Acts 4:12).

Kingdom Outlook

A second principle comes into play when preparing to preach evangelistically from the Old Testament—seeing the purpose of God in creation and redemption consummate in the coming of his kingdom.

God wanted to display his glory, not just on the grandeur of the created universe, but supremely in persons who could know him, and in a relationship of love, enjoy him forever. To this end he made a man and woman in his image and told them to be "fruitful and increase in number; fill the earth and subdue it" (Gen. 1:28).

Though this great commission was seemingly ignored in its spiritual application, God's plan for humanity never changed. He has from the beginning intended to raise up a posterity in his likeness that would populate the earth, a people made beautiful in his holiness who will never cease to praise him (Rev. 7:9–10).

The rebellion of Adam and Eve invoked God's judgment and brought death upon the human race, but it did not alter his purpose for creation. Out of that calamity in the garden, he promised to bring from the "offspring" of the woman one who would "crush" the serpent-like devil (Gen. 3:15), a passage referred to as the protoevangelium. The coming of this future victorious Savior and the ultimate completion of God's plan for the world is assured.

His purpose comes into bold manifestation in the call of Abram to leave his old life and go out with God to a land that will be shown him: "I will make you a great nation, and I will bless you . . . and all peoples on earth will be blessed through you" (Gen. 12:2–3).

The promise was repeated again and again as Abram and Sarah moved out by faith (Gen. 13:14–17; 15:4–21; 17:1–8; 18:1–19; 22:15–18). Later the same prophetic words were spoken to Isaac (Gen. 26:4, 23–24) and repeated to his son Jacob (Gen. 28:14–15; 35:9–12).

Abraham's descendants thus were chosen to be God's witness to the nations. Just as the patriarch had walked circumspectly before the Lord, so his offspring were to live blameless lives. To teach them how this conduct develops, the law was given to Moses. Obedience to these commandments, when motivated by love to God, would make the Israelites uniquely beautiful in their character.

This was God's strategy of evangelism in the Old Testament. The Jews were to be so morally different from the degenerate nations about them that people seeing their holy lifestyle would want to know their Lord. "See, I have made him a witness to the peoples," Isaiah wrote. "You will summon nations you know not, and nations that do not know you will hasten to you, because of the Lord your God, the Holy One of Israel, for he has endowed you with splendor" (Isa. 55:5; cf. Zech. 8:23).

The descendants of Abraham, however, seldom manifested the likeness of their Creator and Lord. More often than not, they were preoccupied with their own indulgent, self-centered ways and forgot the law and their mission. Thankfully, there was always in Israel a remnant that remained faithful. There were also occasional seasons of revival that occurred intermittently through the Old Testament, though they were usually short-lived and engendered little evangelistic concern for the lost nations about them. With the exception of Nineveh—and that only by God's overriding the disobedience of Jonah—there is no indication of revival significantly reaching any Gentile nation.

Nevertheless, God keeps before his people the expectation of a day when his plan for the world through the offspring of Abraham will be realized in the coming of the Messiah who will bring "salvation to the ends of the earth" (Isa. 49:6). "He will reign on David's throne and over his kingdom, establishing and upholding it with justice and righteousness from that time on and forever" (Isa. 9:7).[11]

This kingdom theme runs through Scripture. Of course, God is inherently King over all nations (2 Kings 19:15; Isa. 6:5; Jer. 46:18), but in a special sense he was King of Israel (Exod. 15:17–18; Deut. 33:5; Isa. 43:15), working in their history to show his glory. However, the kingdom never had been fully realized in their experience, though it was prefigured by David.

The anticipated King was acknowledged by Daniel to be "a son of man, coming with the clouds of heaven" who is "given authority, glory and sovereign power; all peoples, nations and men of every language worship him" (Dan. 7:13–14). "The saints of the Most High," he says, "receive the kingdom and will possess it forever—yes, for ever and ever" (Dan. 7:18).

While much about this passage remains unclear, one cannot mistake its dominant note, which is the ultimate triumph of the apocalyptic Son of Man. This was the way Jesus referred most often to himself. Every time he used this name, it was more than a prophecy of his coming rule; it indicated that in his mind that rule was already present. That which had been given in covenant, embodied in the law, typified in Israel's government, and envisioned by the prophets, was fulfilled in his life and work. In him the kingdom had come and was coming.

It is present in the salvation sense of spiritual reality when the King is Lord and served (Luke 17:20–21; cf. 16:16; Matt. 18:3; John 3:5). It is future when the kingdom comes to fruition in the day of the Lord, when the gospel of the kingdom has been preached in all the world for a witness (Matt. 24:14), and the King comes in the clouds of glory to reign over his kingdom forever.

What tremendous opportunities this news opens up for evangelism! Virtually every salvation theme in the Bible comes into view, as history is seen moving toward its goal, when every knee will bow and every tongue confess that Jesus Christ is Lord. Eternity takes hold and the whole sermon is flavored with expectancy, even as it feels the certainty of the coming judgment.

Soul Searching

On this note, a final principle needs attention when preparing to preach evangelistically—the sermon must bring people to see their need of salvation.[12] Is the message soul-searching?

In answering this question, the preacher visualizes the audience for whom the sermon is intended, trying to be sensitive to their situation. A message that hits home must meet people where they are, both in their interests and attitudes respecting the subject. By knowing where they are coming from, the preacher can make the application more direct.[13]

This means rooting out the fundamental problem of sin. Beginning with the fall in the garden, the Old Testament shows mankind in rebellion against God, the creature actually holding the will of the Creator in contempt and worshiping his own works as a false god (Rom. 1:15). Its ultimate expression comes in the defiant rejection of their promised Savior (Isa. 53:3; John 1:10–11).

Such blasphemy cannot be ignored by a just God because it is an affront to his holiness and love. Inevitably, then, the profane must be separated from him. Furthermore, his wrath upon iniquity cannot be annulled as long as the cause of evil remains. Since life is unending, all the spiritual consequences of sin continue on forever in hell.

Knowing, therefore, the terror of the Lord, the preacher strikes at the heart of sin. Urging at one time the greatness of the rebel's guilt and at another the imminence of his doom, he seeks to awaken the human conscience. Innumerable times in the Old Testament the awfulness of sin becomes vivid. Although all the diverse kinds of sin cannot be treated in one message, at least the basic issue of unbelief and disobedience can be disclosed, with perhaps a few specific applications to the immediate situation.

There should never be any confusion about whom the evangelistic preacher is addressing. It is not sin in theory, but the sinner in practice that he is talking about. While, of course, consideration of propriety and good sense must be kept in mind, a good sermon gets under the skin of sinners and makes them squirm under conviction of the Spirit. A message that does not deal with this cause of human woe, individually and collectively, is irrelevant to human need.

Whatever the structure of the sermon, it should follow a convincing course of logic. A good, balanced outline will go a long way toward this end. The points should flow effortlessly out of the passage. Moreover, they should be arranged in such a way that each builds upon the other, creating a progression of thought leading up to the appeal for decision. When this is done well, the invitation seems as natural as it is necessary.

How one chooses to make this appeal will depend upon the circumstances as the Holy Spirit leads.[14] It is something the preacher should give a lot of thought and prayer to in preparing the sermon. An evangelistic message calls for a response, just as God did when he asked our forebears after they sinned in the garden, "Where are you?" (Gen. 3:9).

One of the many ways the Old Testament makes us answer this question comes out in times of great crises. God warns the people of the consequences of continuing in sin, but he offers mercy if they will return to him in true repentance. Tragically, the generation of Noah did not heed the call (Gen. 6:1–7:22; 2 Peter 2:5), nor the inhabitants of Sodom and Gomorrah (Gen. 18:14–19), both instances cited by Jesus as examples of God's judgment upon a rebellious people (Matt. 24:37–39; 10:15). On other occasions, however, when catastrophe threatened, God brought deliverance according to his promise: "If my people, who are called by my name, will humble themselves and pray and seek my face and turn from their wicked ways, then will I hear from heaven and will forgive their sin and will heal their land" (2 Chron. 7:14). Looking into seasons of revival in the Old Testament when people respond to the challenge of this promise offers many applications to the good news of salvation.[15]

One of the best examples of preaching evangelistically from the Old Testament, and surely the most far reaching, is Peter's sermon at Pentecost (Acts 2:14–41).[16] Beginning with the immediate situation, he relates the outpouring of the Holy Spirit to the prophecy of Joel and its application to the gospel: "Everyone who calls on the name of the Lord will be saved" (vv. 16–21; cf. Joel 2:28–32).

After arresting the interest of his audience, he proceeds to lift up the answer to their need of the Savior. He is "Jesus of Nazareth," God identifying with humanity as "a man." His divine credentials were attended among them by "miracles, wonders and signs"—mighty works of which they were fully aware (v. 22).

Then he comes to Calvary, where Jesus was "handed over" to the people. No accident, it was according to "God's set purpose and foreknowledge" that the promised Savior offered himself for the sins of the world (v. 23; cf. Isa. 53:10). Leaving no doubt about who was responsible, Peter goes on to say, "And you, with the help of wicked men, put him to death by nailing him to the cross" (v. 23).

Having made clear their guilt, while declaring the fact of Christ's voluntary atoning sacrifice, the preacher now triumphantly exclaims, "But God raised him from the dead, freeing him from the agony of death, because it was impossible for death to keep its hold on him" (v. 24). What an awe-inspiring announcement!

Elaborating on this pivotal truth, he quotes at length from the Psalms, noting what David, "seeing what was ahead," had foretold: "The resurrection of the Christ, that he was not abandoned to the grave, nor did his body see decay" (vv. 25–31; cf. Ps. 16:8–11). To this Old Testament witness, Peter adds his own personal testimony, an experience shared by the other apostles (v. 32).

The exalting of Jesus continues with his ascension to the throne of heaven, where he has taken authority at "the right hand of God," and "received from the Father the promised Holy Spirit," which he has "poured out" on them (v. 33). Further strengthening his point, Peter observes that Christ's reign stands in contrast to that of David, who did not ascend to heaven, though he wrote, "The Lord said to my Lord: 'Sit at my right hand until I make your enemies a footstool for your feet'" (vv. 34–35; cf. Ps. 110:1). With this resounding affirmation of the sacred writings cherished by his Jewish audience, Peter now boldly declared, "Therefore let all Israel be assured of this: God has made this Jesus, whom you crucified, both Lord and Christ" (v. 36).

These words fall upon the people with such conviction that "they were cut to the heart." Feeling the weight of their sin, the crowd cries out to the evangelist and his associates, "Brothers, what shall we do?" (v. 37).

At this point Peter extends the invitation, calling upon his hearers to "repent and be baptized in the name of Jesus Christ."

In return they would receive "forgiveness" of their sins and the renewing "gift of the Holy Spirit" (v. 38). So the sermon leads to the promise of a new life freely given to all who truly believe. Better still, the invitation does not apply only to those persons gathered in Jerusalem that day, but it includes their "children," and extends even to those "who are far off—for all whom the Lord our God will call" (v. 39).

Yet, wonderful as the invitation sounds, Peter does not close without some solemn words of warning to persons who do not heed the gospel call. There is startling realism in his voice, born out of deep compassion, as he pleads, like the prophets of old, "Save yourselves from this corrupt generation" (v. 40).

Whatever one may think of this kind of preaching, it is what gave birth to the New Testament church. And I might add, we need a lot more of it today.

In preparing to preach this way, I think of Robert Murray McCheyne, a much beloved exponent of God's Word of a past generation. A few years after the death of the famous preacher, a young minister visited his church to discover, as he explained, the secret of the man's tremendous influence. The sexton, who had served under Mr. McCheyne, took the youthful inquirer into the vestry and asked him to sit in the chair used by the great preacher.

"Now put your elbows on the table," he said. "Now put your face in your hands." The visitor obeyed. "Now let the tears fall down. That was the way Mr. McCheyne used to do!"

The man then led the minister to the pulpit and gave a fresh series of instructions. "Put your elbows down on the pulpit!" He put his elbows down. "Now put your face in your hands!" He did as he was told. "Now let the tears fall down. That was the way Mr. McCheyne used to do!"[17]

Yes, that is the way to do it. Not that physical tears must fall, but that the compassion which they represent should characterize every preacher, feeling the weight of lost souls, knowing that their destiny may hang upon his sermon. Above every other consideration, it is this passion that everyone come to Christ and partake of eternal life that makes evangelistic preaching consistent with its mission.

The old patriarchs of Harvard may not have been homileticians, but they were thinking like evangelistic preachers when they laid down the Laws, Liberties, and Orders of the college. Unfortunately, their rebel aspirations were largely forgotten in subsequent generations, but what they said still holds true, especially for ministers of the gospel preparing to preach evangelistically: "Everyone shall consider the main end of his life and studies is to know God and Jesus Christ, which is eternal life."[18]

Questions to Consider

1. What does the author say makes a sermon uniquely evangelistic?
2. How does being Christ-centered fit into evangelistic preaching from the Old Testament?
3. What does it mean to have a kingdom outlook?
4. How does a preacher make sermons soul-searching?
5. How can you make a difference in your ministry by preaching evangelistic sermons from the Old Testament?

On the Shelf

Graham, Billy, et. al. *Choose Ye This Day: How to Effectively Proclaim the Gospel Message.* Minneapolis: World Wide Publications, 1989.

Kaiser, Walter C., Jr. *The Christian and the "Old" Testament.* Pasadena: William Carey Library, 1998.

Larsen, David. *The Evangelistic Mandate.* Grand Rapids: Kregel, 1992.

Richard, Ramesh. *Preaching Evangelistic Sermons.* Grand Rapids: Baker, 2005.

Perry, Lloyd M., and John H. Strubhar. *Evangelistic Preaching.* Chicago: Moody, 1979.

Street, R. Alan. *The Effective Invitation.* Old Tappan, NJ: Revell, 1984.

Afterword

Preaching the Old Testament

Scott M. Gibson

In the preface to his important work on biblical exegesis, Walter Kaiser remarks, "I have been aware for some time now of a gap that has existed in academic preparation for ministry. It is the gap that exists between the study of the biblical text (most frequently in the original languages of Hebrew, Aramaic, and Greek) and the actual delivery of messages to God's people."[1] This book is another contribution to bridging the gap about which Kaiser is concerned. In addition, this book serves as a tribute to Walter Kaiser, who has made it one of his chief goals to stand in the gap by providing scholarship and modeling for generations of preachers who struggle with exegesis as they prepare to preach from the Old Testament.

Throughout this book the authors have helped preachers gain the necessary materials for filling in the gap as they put into practice their Hebrew, as they engage in the exegesis of various books and genres, as they try to understand more fully the cultural background of the Old Testament, as they gain perspective on the relationship between the two Testaments, and as they perceive the importance of preaching the Old Testament today, to real people, hundreds of years separated from the days of the patriarchs.

All of the chapters in this book come from the commitment that the entire Bible is our authority and we are called to preach the entire counsel of God. Walter C. Kaiser Jr. has demonstrated this commitment in his teaching, writing, and preaching. As an Old Testament scholar, he often preaches from the New Testament and, as he teasingly quips, "I like it. It comes after the Old Testament."

Both Testaments are important. One is not to be preached to the exclusion of the other. For decades Walter C. Kaiser Jr. has helped pastors and teachers gain an appreciation for the Old Testament and the skills to preach it with confidence and grace. The chapters in this book are written by a few of Kaiser's friends and colleagues who wanted to express to him—and to God—their appreciation for what God has done in and through this servant, Walter C. Kaiser Jr.

If preachers take seriously the preaching of the Old Testament, they might agree with the pastor who observed, "Because the cultural setting of the Old Testament is further removed from us than certain New Testament passages, it may be more difficult to preach. But, if a pastor digs hard for both the hermeneutical and homiletical ideas, I believe that the Old Testament will serve as wonderful preaching material." This book helps preachers to do just that: recognize that the Old Testament is a wonder, a delightful wonder, from which preachers can preach astounding ideas. And that has been the purpose of this book, to prepare preachers to preach the Old Testament. Preach the Word—all of it!

Notes

Foreword

1. John Walton and Andrew Hill, *Old Testament Today* (Grand Rapids: Zondervan, 2004), xiii.

2. Barbara Brown Taylor, "Preaching the Terrors," *Journal for Preachers* 15, no. 2 (1992): 3.

3. Elizabeth Achtemeier, *Preaching Hard Texts of the Old Testament* (Peabody, MA: Hendrickson, 1998), xi.

Introduction: Kaiser Is the Key Word

1. Walter C. Kaiser Jr., *Toward an Exegetical Theology: Biblical Exegesis for Preaching and Teaching* (Grand Rapids: Baker, 1981), 155–56.

Chapter 2: Keeping Your Hebrew Healthy

1. David W. Baker and Elaine A. Heath [with Morven R. Baker], *More Light on the Path* (Grand Rapids: Baker, 1998), 5.

2. Among scores of publications, one of the groundbreaking works on learning styles through multisensory modality approaches was Rita Dunn and Kenneth Dunn, *Teaching Students through Their Individual Learning Styles* (Reston, VA: Prentice-Hall, 1978); Gregorc's model of learning styles is presented in his definitive volume, Anthony D. Gregorc, *An Adult's Guide to Style* (Columbia, CT: Gregorc Associates, 1982); also, Gordon Lawrence, *People Types and Tiger Stripes: A Practical Guide to Learning Styles*, 2nd ed. (Gainesville, FL: Center for Application of Psychological Types, 1982); Gardner's theory of seven intelligences, Howard Gardner, *Frames of Mind* (New York: Basic Books, 1983); Thomas Armstrong, *In Their Own Way: Discovering and Encouraging Your Child's Personal Learning Style* (New York: St. Martin's Press, 1987); Kathleen Butler, *It's All in Your Mind: A Student's Guide to Learning Style* (Columbia, CT: The Learner's Dimension, 1988); Cynthia Ulrich Tobias and Pat Guild, *No Sweat: How to Use Your Learning Style to Be a Better Student* (Seattle: The Teaching Advisory, 1991);

Thomas Armstrong, *7 Kinds of Smart* (New York: Penguin Books, 1993); Cynthia Ulrich Tobias, *The Way They Learn* (Colorado Springs: Focus on the Family, 1994).

3. Miles V. Van Pelt and Gary D. Pratico, *The Vocabulary Guide to Biblical Hebrew* (Grand Rapids: Zondervan, 2003), ix.

4. Francis I. Andersen and A. Dean Forbes, *The Vocabulary of the Old Testament* (Rome: Pontifical Biblical Institute, 1992), 8.

5. Van Pelt and Pratico, *Vocabulary Guide*, ix.

6. Larry A. Mitchel, *A Student's Vocabulary for Biblical Hebrew and Aramaic* (Grand Rapids: Zondervan, 1984).

7. George M. Landes, *Building Your Biblical Hebrew Vocabulary: Learning Words by Frequency and Cognate* (Atlanta: Society of Biblical Literature, 2001).

8. Landes, *Building Your Biblical Hebrew Vocabulary*, ix.

9. Ibid.

10. See note 3 above.

11. Miles V. Van Pelt, *Old Testament Hebrew Vocabulary Cards* (Grand Rapids: Zondervan, 2003).

12. Mark D. Futato, *Beginning Biblical Hebrew* (Winona Lake, IN: Eisenbrauns, 2003).

13. Allen P. Ross, *Introducing Biblical Hebrew* (Grand Rapids: Baker, 2001).

14. Choon Leong Seow, *A Grammar for Biblical Hebrew* (Nashville: Abingdon, 1987).

15. Jonathan T. Pennington, *Old Testament Hebrew Vocabulary*, Audio CD (Grand Rapids: Zondervan, 2003).

16. BibleWorks, HERMENEUTIKA, P.O. Box 2200, Big Fork, MT 59911-2200, PH: 800-74-BIBLE; FAX: 406-837-4433; http://www.bibleworks.com.

17. Van Pelt and Pratico, *Vocabulary Guide*, xii.

18. *Hebrew Tutor for Multimedia CD-ROM*. Parsons Technology.

19. Donald R. Vance, *A Hebrew Reader for Ruth* (Peabody, MA: Hendrickson, 2003).

20. Gary A. Long, *Grammatical Concepts 101 for Biblical Hebrew: Learning Biblical Hebrew Grammatical Concepts Through English Grammar* (Peabody, MA: Hendrickson, 2002).

21. Ehud Ben Zvi, Maxine Hancock, and Richard Beinert, *Readings in Biblical Hebrew: An Intermediate Textbook* (New Haven: Yale University Press, 1993).

22. Bonnie Pedrotti Kittel, Vicki Hoffer, and Rebecca Abts Wright, *Biblical Hebrew: A Text and Workbook* (New Haven: Yale University Press, 1989).

23. Moshe Greenberg, *Introduction to Hebrew* (Englewood Cliffs: Prentice-Hall, 1965).

24. Page H. Kelley, *Biblical Hebrew: An Introductory Grammar* (Grand Rapids: Eerdmans, 1992).

25. Thomas O. Lambdin, *Introduction to Biblical Hebrew* (New York: Charles Scribner's Sons, 1971).

26. See note 14 above.

27. Jacob Weingreen, *A Practical Grammar for Classical Hebrew*, 2nd ed. (Oxford: Clarendon Press, 1959).

28. Emil Friedrich Kautzsch, ed., *Gesenius' Hebrew Grammar*, 2nd English ed., revised in accordance with the 28th German ed. (1909) by Arthur Ernest Cowley (Oxford: Clarendon Press, 1970).

29. Paul Joüon, *A Grammar of Biblical Hebrew*, Subsidia Biblica, 14, translated and revised by T. Muraoka, 2 vols. (Rome: Editrice Pontificio Instituto Biblico, 1993).

30. Bruce K. Waltke and M. O'Connor, *An Introduction to Biblical Hebrew Syntax* (Winona Lake, IN: Eisenbrauns, 1990).

31. Christo H. J. van der Merwe, Jackie A. Naudé, and Jan H. Kroeze, *A Biblical Hebrew Reference Grammar*, Biblical Languages: Hebrew, 3 (Sheffield, UK: Sheffield Academic Press, 1999).

32. Bill T. Arnold and John H. Choi, *A Guide to Biblical Hebrew Syntax* (Cambridge: Cambridge University Press, 2003).

33. Ibid., xi.

34. See note 30 above.

35. Robert B. Chisholm Jr., *From Exegesis to Exposition: A Practical Guide to Using Biblical Hebrew* (Grand Rapids: Baker, 1998), 31–147; also Ronald J. Williams, *Hebrew Syntax: An Outline*, 2nd ed. (Toronto: University of Toronto Press, 1976).

36. Susan Anne Groom, *Linguistic Analysis of Biblical Hebrew* (Waynesboro, GA: Paternoster Press, 2003).

37. Van der Merwe, *A Biblical Hebrew Reference Grammar*, 9.

38. Jessica W. Goldstein, *The First Hebrew Reader: Guided Selections from the Hebrew Bible* (Berkeley, CA: EKS Publishing Co., 2000); Jessica W. Goldstein, *The First Hebrew Reader: Guided Selections from the Hebrew Bible, Companion Audio CD* (Berkeley, CA: EKS Publishing Co., 2002).

39. Randall Buth, *Living Biblical Hebrew for Everyone*, 2 vols. (Jerusalem: Biblical Language Center, 2003); and Randall Buth, *Living Biblical Hebrew: Selected Readings with 500 Friends* (Jerusalem: Biblical Language Center, 2005).

40. Buth credits Harry Winitz's picture series "Learnables" for modern languages, James Asher's breakthrough with his "Total Physical Response," and the "comprehensible input" factor for natural language acquisition explained by Stephen Krashen.

41. *The Hebrew Bible Narrated*, http://www.jewishsoftware.com.

42. "Hebrew Old Testament" MP3–CD, Audio Scriptures International, P.O. Box 460634, Escondido, CA, www.audioscriptures.org.

43. Pesach Goldberg, trans., *The Linear Chumash*, vol. 1, *Bereshis* (Jerusalem: Feldheim Publishers, 1992–1997); Pesach Goldberg, trans., *The Linear Chumash*, vol. 2, *Shemosh* (Jerusalem: Feldheim Publishers, 1987); Pesach Goldberg, trans., *The Linear Chumash*, vol. 3, *Vayikro* (Jerusalem: Feldheim Publishers, 1992–1997); Pesach Goldberg, trans., *The Linear Chumash*, vol. 4, *Bemidbar* (Jerusalem: Feldheim Publishers, 1997); Pesach Goldberg, trans., *The Linear Chumash*, vol. 5, *Devorim* (Jerusalem: Feldheim Publishers, 1992–1997).

44. Pesach Goldberg, trans., *The Linear Megillos: Esther* (Jerusalem: Feldheim Publishers, 1997).

45. Heinrich Bitzer, ed., *Light on the Path: Daily Scripture Readings in Hebrew and Greek*, vol. 1 (Marburg: Oekumenischer Verlag, Dr. R. F. Edel, 1969; Grand Rapids: Baker, 1982); Heinrich Bitzer, ed., *Light on the Path: Daily Scripture Readings in Hebrew and Greek*, vol. 2 (Marburg: Oekumenischer Verlag, Dr. R. F. Edel, 1973).

46. See note 1 above.

47. Bitzer, *Light on the Path*, vol. 1, 10.

48. *Gramcord*, The Gramcord Institute, 2218 NE Brookview Dr., Vancouver, WA 98686, PH: 360-576-3000; FAX: 503-761-0626; http://www.gramcord.org.

49. See note 16 above.

50. Francis Brown, S. R. Driver, and Charles A. Briggs, eds., *The New Brown-Driver-Briggs Hebrew and English Lexicon (Complete and Unabridged Electronic Edition)*, Varda Books, 2004. http://www.publishersrow.com/ebookshuk/.

51. http://www.publishersrow.com/ebookshuk/.

52. Ludwig Koehler and Walter Baumgartner, eds., *The Hebrew and Aramaic Lexicon of the Old Testament*, 4 vols., revised ed., trans. and ed. under the supervision of M. E. J. Richardson [CD-ROM Edition] (Leiden: Brill, 1994–2001).

53. Frederic Clarke Putnam, comp., *A Cumulative Index to the Grammar and Syntax of Biblical Hebrew* (Winona Lake, IN: Eisenbrauns, 1996).

Chapter 3: Preaching from the Historical Books

1. The Hebrew Bible is divided into three sections: the Law, Prophets, and Writings. The books of Joshua, Judges, Samuel, and Kings are included in the Prophets, whereas Ruth, Esther, Ezra, Nehemiah, and Chronicles are included in the Writings.

2. See C. G. Bartholomew and M. W. Goheen, *The Drama of Scripture: Finding Our Place in the Biblical Story* (Grand Rapids: Baker, 2004), and also N. T. Wright, *The New Testament and the People of God* (Minneapolis: Fortress Press, 1992).

3. Since the genre of the historical books is "narrative," the chapter in this volume by Jeffrey D. Arthurs, "Preaching the Old Testament Narratives," provides helpful insights into how to identify important narrative features in a story. See also Robert Alter, *The Art of Biblical Narrative* (New York: Basic Books, 1981) and Walter C. Kaiser's chapter on "Preaching and Teaching Narrative Texts of the Old Testament" in *Preaching and Teaching from the Old Testament: A Guide for the Church* (Grand Rapids: Baker, 2003), 63–82.

4. For example, see Gen. 12:7; 13:14–17; 17:8.

5. Understanding the role and function of the covenants is especially important for understanding the larger narrative context of the Old Testament since the covenants provide the theological framework for God's redemptive story. One helpful book is by W. Dumbrell, *Covenant and Creation: A Theology of Old Testament Covenants* (Grand Rapids: Baker, 1993).

6. For example, see Exod. 20:3–5; 34:14–17; Deut. 4:16–18, 23–28; 5:7–9.

7. The story is also recorded in 2 Kings 18:17–19:37 and in Isaiah 36–37.

8. Resources to help you with historical research are listed at the conclusion of this chapter.

9. For pictures of Lachish and the archaeology of Tel Lachish, see D. Ussishkin, *The Conquest of Lachish by Sennacherib* (Tel Aviv: Tel Aviv University, 1982).

10. "Prism of Sennacherib," translated by A. L. Oppenheim, in *Ancient Near Eastern Texts*, ed. J. B. Pritchard (Princeton: Princeton University Press, 1969), 288.

Chapter 4: Preaching the Old Testament Narratives

1. Cicero, *Orator*, in George A. Kennedy, *Classical Rhetoric and Its Christian and Secular Tradition from Ancient to Modern Times* (Chapel Hill, NC: University of North Carolina Press, 1980), 100.

2. Gordon D. Fee and Douglas Stuart, *How to Read the Bible for All Its Worth: A Guide to Understanding the Bible*, 2nd ed. (Grand Rapids: Zondervan, 1982), 74–75.

3. See Sidney Greidanus, *Preaching Christ from the Old Testament* (Grand Rapids: Eerdmans, 1999), and Bryan Chapell, *Christ-Centered Preaching: Redeeming the Expository Sermon*, 2nd ed. (Grand Rapids: Baker, 2004).

4. Bernard Ramm, *Protestant Biblical Interpretation*, 3rd ed. (Grand Rapids: Baker, 1985), 113.

5. Eric Auerbach, *Mimesis: The Representation of Reality in Western Literature*, trans. Willard Trask (Princeton: Princeton University Press, 1953), 14–15.

6. Dale Patrick and Allen Scult, *Rhetoric and Biblical Interpretation* (Sheffield, UK: Almond, 1990), 29.

7. John Sailhamer, *Introduction to Old Testament Theology* (Grand Rapids: Baker, 1995), 46–47.

8. Shimon Bar-Efrat, *Narrative Art in the Bible* (Sheffield, UK: Almond, 1989), 93.

9. Aristotle, *The Poetics*, trans. Ingram Bywater (New York: Modern Library), 1450b.

10. Don Sunukjian, "A Night In Persia," in *Biblical Sermons: How Twelve Preachers Apply the Principles of Biblical Preaching*, ed. Haddon Robinson (Grand Rapids: Baker, 1989), 71–80.

11. Henry Grady Davis, *Design for Preaching* (Philadelphia: Fortress, 1958), 157.

12. Paul Aurandt, *Paul Harvey's The Rest of the Story* (New York: Bantam, 1977); *More of Paul Harvey's The Rest of the Story* (New York: Bantam, 1980); *Destiny* (New York: Bantam, 1983).

13. Sydney Greidanus, *The Modern Preacher and the Ancient Text: Interpreting and Preaching Biblical Literature* (Grand Rapids: Eerdmans, 1988), 225.

14. Haddon Robinson, *Biblical Preaching: The Development and Delivery of Expository Messages*, 2nd ed. (Grand Rapids: Baker, 2001), 130–31.

15. Bar-Efrat, *Narrative Art in the Bible*, 148.

16. Richard L. Pratt, *He Gave Us Stories: The Bible Student's Guide to Interpreting Old Testament Narratives* (Brentwood, TN: Wolgemuth & Hyatt, 1990), 138–39.

17. Ibid., 147.

18. Eugene Peterson, *Leap Over a Wall: Earthly Spirituality for Everyday Christians* (New York: HarperCollins, 1997), 76.

19. Northrop Frye, *The Great Code: The Bible and Literature* (New York: Harcourt Brace, 1982); John Sailhamer, *The Pentateuch as Narrative* (Grand Rapids: Zondervan, 1992); cf. *Introduction to Old Testament Theology*.

Chapter 5: Preaching from the Law

1. Parts of this essay will also appear within the author's forthcoming commentary on Exodus in the New American Commentary (Nashville: Broadman and Holman).

2. Consider, for example, laws against incest. They are delineated in the Old Testament (Leviticus 18) but simply assumed in the New Testament (1 Cor. 5:1–5). Paul doesn't need to restate them, but only to give instructions on the basis of them—instructions that obviously assume their continuing validity as indicators of the will of God for how his people should behave.

3. This is precisely what Yahweh did for Israel: they were not on equal terms with him, but took instead the role of vassals to a suzerain, a great king who spared them and then gave them the terms under which they could enjoy his benefits if they kept his commands.

4. In the Deuteronomy covenant, the primary witness to the covenant is Yahweh, but "heaven and earth" and "these words" and "you yourselves" are also found as secondary or backup witnesses. In Exodus-Leviticus, however, it is Yahweh who is the exclusive witness. Therefore, he is both the main character of the preamble as well

as of the witness list, in contrast to the usual situation in other ancient Near Eastern covenants, where the king is the main character in the preamble, and various gods are the primary witnesses. Such a polytheistic approach would be completely out of place in Yahweh's covenant, which recognizes both explicitly and implicitly his sole divinity and ultimate kingship.

5. The supplemental instructions in Numbers are not secondary in importance; they are more like the various amendments to the Constitution of the United States, which include the famous Bill of Rights. Many of the laws in Numbers were indeed revealed by God after the Israelites left Sinai, but not as secondary "afterthoughts." They were, rather, a variety of statutes memorably imposed during the wilderness wanderings in response to specific needs as they arose.

6. As Eckart Otto points out ("Korperverletzung in hethitischen und israelitischen Recht: Rechts- und religionhistorische Aspekte," *Religiongeschichtliche Beziehungen zwischen Kleinasien, Nordsyrien und dem Alten Testament*, Orbis biblicus et orientalis 129, ed. B. Janowski et al. [Freiburg: Universitätsverlag, 1993], 391–425), one very distinct and obvious difference between the Israelite covenant law and the somewhat similar laws found among the Hittites and Mesopotamians is simply the way that Israelite law consistently declares its origins in God, whereas the other laws take their authority from a king. This king is considered to be acting in the role of a mediator of the law on behalf of a divine figure, but is nevertheless the promulgator of the law, which does not come directly from a god or goddess.

7. A number of scholars have challenged the idea that the Exodus-Leviticus and Deuteronomic covenants reflect the structure of the second-millennium treaty covenants of the ancient Near East, a connection that had been convincingly promulgated by Mendenhall (George E. Mendenhall, *Law and Covenant in Israel and the Ancient Near East* [Pittsburgh: Presbyterian Board of Colportage, 1955], also in *Biblical Archaeologist* 17 [1954]: 26–46, 49–76). Mendenhall has updated his conclusions in his article, coauthored with Gary Herion, in the *Anchor Bible Dictionary* ("Covenant"), in which he suggests that the presentation of the form in the Bible is somewhat altered to reflect neo-Assyrian elements, but still preserves elements that can only be second-millennium in provenance. Our position holds that the elements thought to be neo-Assyrian (that is, those not exactly typical of second-millennium treaties) are simply the specific Israelite adaptations made by Yahweh through Moses, rather than having late extrabiblical origins at all. See also Robert D. Miller II, "Moses and Mendenhall in Traditio-Historical Perspective," *Irish Biblical Studies* 23 (2001): 146–66.

8. Though it is possible that the Ten Commandments/Words are so described later by God himself. See the commentaries on Exod. 24:12.

9. From W. L. Moran's article "The Ancient Near Eastern Background of the Love of God in Deuteronomy" (*Catholic Biblical Quarterly* 77 [1963]: 77–87) come the following citations demonstrating the idiomatic sense of "loving" God and "loving" neighbor as self. To love in such contexts does not refer primarily to emotional attachment, but rather to active *loyalty*, to a commitment to be someone's ally and supporter regardless of how one might "feel" about that person:

1. G. Dossin, *Archives royales de Mari* V 76:4 (To Yasmi`-Adad, King of Mari, 18th c. BC [writer of the letter unknown]) "I am the king's servant and the one who *loves* you."
2. J. A. Knudtzon, *Die El-Amarna Tafeln* [*El Amarna*] 53:40–44 (Tushratta, king of Mitanni, to the Pharaoh) "My lord, just as I *love* the king my lord, so do

the king of Nuhashshe, the king of Ni'i . . .—all these kings are servants of my lord."

3. *El Amarna* 114:68 (Rib-Addi of Byblos to the Pharaoh) "Who will *love* if I die?"
4. *El Amarna* 138:71–73 (Rib-Addi of Byblos to the Pharaoh) "Behold the city! Half of it *loves* the sons of Abdi-Ashirta, half of it my lord."
5. *El Amarna* 83:47–51 (Rib-Addi of Byblos to the Pharaoh) "If you send me no answer, I will leave the city and go away with the people who *love* me."
6. D. J. Wiseman, *Iraq* 20 (1958) 49 col. iv 266–68 (Esarhaddon to various vassal kings requiring them to be loyal to his son and successor Assurbanipal) "You will *love* Assurbanipal as yourselves."
7. L. Waterman, *Royal Correspondence of the Assyrian Empire* 266, 1105:32 (Oath imposed by Assurbanipal on his vassal kings just before going to war with Shamash-shum-ukin, his brother, in Babylon) "The king of Assyria, our lord, we will *love*."
8. 1 Kings 5:15 [English 5:1] "Because Hiram had been a *lover* of David all his life" (*ki 'oher haya chiram ledawid kol hayamin*).

10. Luke 10:25–28, Mark 12:28–34, and Matt. 19:19 suggest that Jesus routinely taught the hierarchy of commandments, Deut. 6:5 and Lev. 19:18 being primary, and the Ten Commandments following as explications of the two.

11. Traditional Judaism counts 613 commandments in the rest of the Pentateuch. Following this enumeration, all the others are 601 in number. There really aren't 613 commandments per se, but the count has been considered a convenient way of giving the impression of the overall quantity.

12. On the lack of citation from law codes in ancient Old Testament–era jurisprudence, even though these law codes were consulted regularly for guidance in rendering legal decisions, see G. R. Driver and J. C. Miles, *The Babylonian Laws* (Oxford: Clarendon, 1952); F. R. Kraus, "Ein zentrales Problem des altmisopotamischen Rechts: Was ist der Codex Hammu-rabi?" *Geneva* 8 (1960): 283–96; Hans Jochen Boecker, *Law and the Administration of Justice in the Bible and the Ancient Near East* (Minneapolis: Augsburg, 1980); Bernard M. Levinson, ed., *Theory and Method in Biblical and Cuneiform Law: Revision, Interpolation, and Development*, *Journal for the Study of the Old Testament* Supplement Series, 181 (Sheffield, UK: Sheffield Academic Press, 1994); Donald B. Redford, "The So-Called 'Codification' of Egyptian Law Under Darius I," in *Persia and Torah: The Theory of Imperial Authorization of the Pentateuch*, ed. James W. Watts, Society of Biblical Literature Symposium Series 17 (Atlanta: Society of Biblical Literature, 2001).

13. It was no accident that judges were selected and in place already in Exodus 18, before the covenant was even given to the Israelites. Without judges to extrapolate from the guiding principles of the law, the application of the covenant stipulations would have been impossible. Judges apply the principles found in the paradigms to the specific situations brought to them in court cases and render verdicts that are in accord with the guidelines of the law, but not necessarily verdicts that are actually mentioned verbatim in the law, since the cases themselves are not necessarily exactly those described in the samplings that the law provides.

14. An obvious parallel in the New Testament is Paul's lists of gifts in Romans 12 and 1 Corinthians 12. Some gifts are very narrow in scope; others are very broad. Moreover, the two lists are not identical (any more than the laws of Exodus-Leviticus

and Deuteronomy are identical). But as a paradigm for the entire corpus of gifts, Paul's lists eloquently tell the reader that any and all special abilities that a person has been given by God that could help build up his church should be employed to that end.

Chapter 6: Preaching from the Psalms and Proverbs

1. Duane A. Garrett, *Proverbs, Ecclesiastes, and Song of Songs*, New American Commentary (Nashville: Broadman Press, 1993), 248.

2. Ibid., 46–48, 116–243.

Chapter 7: Preaching from the Prophets

1. Few evangelical biblical scholars have devoted more attention to this subject than Walter C. Kaiser Jr. I am honored to offer these comments on preparing to preach from the prophets in appreciation for his friendship and as an acknowledgment of his many contributions to the subject.

2. Contra the excellent book by William M. Schniedewind, *How the Bible Became a Book* (Cambridge: Cambridge University Press, 2004). Schniedewind argues, along with the majority of biblical scholars, that making the Bible a book was the work of the priesthood and its scribal guild.

3. John H. Sailhamer, "Biblical Theology and the Composition of the Hebrew Bible," *Biblical Theology, Retrospect and Prospect*, ed. Scott J. Hafemann (Downers Grove, IL: InterVarsity, 2002), 26–37.

4. Our discussion of "books" at this early period should not be read anachronistically in terms of the modern sense of a "book," but as a general designation of the form given to ancient written documents of many types.

5. Isaiah 8:20 (NASB): "To the law and to the testimony! If they do not speak according to this word, it is because they have no dawn."

6. "If in reply it is asked whether Christianity is really a book-religion, the answer is that strangely enough Christianity has always been and only been a living religion when it is not ashamed to be actually and seriously a book-religion." Karl Barth, *Church Dogmatics*, Vol. 1, pt. 2 (Edinburgh: T & T Clark, 1978), 494–95.

7. This is the same covenant that Christ made with the church (Luke 22:20). See John H. Sailhamer, *The Pentateuch as Narrative: A Biblical-Theological Commentary* (Grand Rapids: Zondervan, 1992).

8. By the expression "earlier" I have tried to avoid the confusion of these prophetic books with the "Early Prophets" of the Hebrew Canon.

9. John H. Sailhamer, "Hosea 11:1 and Matthew 2:15," *Westminster Theological Journal* 63 (2001): 87–96.

10. Hengstenberg noted that "in history the Messianic hopes of the nation always assume the appearance of an echo only" and that "they seem to have been introduced from above into the spirit of the nation, and that each particular element was to be found in a prophetic communication, before it took possession of the mind of the nation." Hengstenberg's concept of an "echo" of divine revelation was one of the foundational insights of his monumental three-volume study of biblical theology which he entitled *Christology of the Old Testament* (1836–1839). Hengstenberg believed that in the composition of the books of the Old Testament there was considerable interdependence among the authors of the individual books. The message of the prophets rested heavily on the central themes of the Pentateuch as well as on each other.

11. Kaiser, *Toward an Exegetical Theology*, 186.

12. A recent study on the importance of the Bible as a "book" is Schniedewind, *How the Bible Became a Book* (see note 2 above).

13. See a similar focus on the prophets and the Pentateuch in Hans-Christoph Schmitt, "Redaktion des Pentateuch im Geiste der Prophetie," *Vetus Testamentum* 32 (1982): 170–89.

14. See Sailhamer, "Biblical Theology and the Composition of the Hebrew Bible" (see note 3 above).

15. Abraham J. Heschel, *The Prophets* (New York: Harper Torchbooks, 1962).

16. Jonah 3:4: *'od 'arba'im yom wninwe nehpakhet.*

17. Christopher R. Seitz, "On Letting a Text 'Act Like a Man,' The Book of the Twelve: New Horizons for Canonical Reading, with Hermeneutical Reflections." This article will appear in a forthcoming book entitled *Prophecy and Hermeneutics: The Twelve and Isaiah in Canonical Introduction*, in the new series, Studies in Theological Interpretation, edited by Craig Bartholomew, Joel Green, and Christopher R. Seitz and published by Baker.

18. Author's own translation.

19. See Sailhamer, *Redaktion des Pentateuch im Geiste der Prophetie*, 1–79.

20. Schmitt, "Redaktion des Pentateuch im Geiste der Prophetie," 170–89

21. John 20:31 says, "But these have been written that you may believe that Jesus is the Christ, the Son of God; and that believing you may have life in His name" (NASB).

22. David W. Baker, "Israelite Prophets and Prophecy," *The Face of Old Testament Studies: A Survey of Contemporary Approaches*, ed. David W. Baker and Bill T. Arnold (Grand Rapids: Baker, 1999), 268–69.

23. John H. Sailhamer, "What Is the Role of History in Biblical Interpretation?" *The Journal of the Evangelical Theological Society* 44, no. 2 (June 2001): 193–206.

24. The expressions denoting these various categories appear similar to those discussed by David W. Baker in the article listed in note 22 (see p. 267), though the content and sense of the categories are very different.

25. Milton S. Terry, *Biblical Hermeneutics* (1883; repr., Grand Rapids: Zondervan, 1979), 231.

26. William M. Schniedewind, *The Word of God in Transition: From Prophet to Exegete in the Second Temple Period*, Journal for the Study of the Old Testament: Supplement Series 197 (Sheffield, UK: Sheffield Academic Press, 1995); David W. Baker, "Scribes as Transmitters of Tradition," *Faith, Tradition, and History: Old Testament Historiography in Its Near Eastern Context*, ed. A. R. Millard, J. K. Hoffmeier, and D. W. Baker (Winona Lake, IN: Eisenbrauns, 1994).

27. "Die Nachgeschichte alttestamentlicher Texts innerhalb des Alten Testaments," Beiheft 66 zur *Zeitschrift für die alttestamentliche Wissenschaft*, 1936, 110–21. Reprinted in *Beiträge zur Traditionsgeschichte und Theologie des Alten Testaments* (Göttingen: Vandenhoeck & Ruprecht, 1962), 69–80.

28. Two recent and helpful studies in this regard are Schniedewind, *How the Bible Became a Book* (see note 2 above) and Christopher R. Seitz, "On Letting a Text 'Act Like a Man,' The Book of the Twelve: New Horizons for Canonical Reading, with Hermeneutical Reflections" (see note 17 above).

Chapter 8: Preaching the Old Testament in Light of Its Culture

1. Walter C. Kaiser Jr., *Hard Sayings of the Old Testament* (Downers Grove, IL: InterVarsity, 1988).

2. J. Scott Duvall and J. Daniel Hays, *Grasping God's Word* (Grand Rapids: Zondervan, 2001).

3. James M. Monson, *Regions on the Run* (Rockford, IL: Biblical Backgrounds, 1998).

4. Ibid.

5. See www.bibback.com.

6. Richard Cleave, *The Holy Land Satellite Atlas*, 2 vols. (Nicosia, Cyprus: Rohr Productions, 1999).

7. See www.preservingbibletimes.org.

8. See www.bibleplaces.com.

9. Walter Brueggemann, *The Land* (Philadelphia: Fortress, 1977), 45–70.

10. Alfred J. Hoerth, *Archaeology and the Old Testament* (Grand Rapids: Baker, 1998).

11. Amihai Mazar, *Archaeology of the Land of the Bible: 10,000–586 B.C.E.* (New York: Doubleday, 1990). See also the *Archaeological Commentary on the Bible* by G. Baez-Carmago (Garden City, NY: Doubleday, 1984).

12. James Bennett Pritchard, ed., *Ancient Near Eastern Texts Relating to the Old Testament*, 3rd ed. (Princeton: Princeton University Press, 1969).

13. Victor H. Matthews and Don C. Benjamin, *Old Testament Parallels: Laws and Stories from the Ancient Near East* (New York: Paulist, 1991).

14. William W. Hallo and K. Lawson Younger, ed., *The Context of Scripture*, 3 vols. (Leiden: Brill, 1997–2002).

15. Walter C. Kaiser Jr., *A History of Israel: From the Bronze Age through the Jewish Wars* (Nashville: Broadman & Holman, 1998).

16. V. Philips Long, *The Art of Biblical History* (Grand Rapids: Zondervan, 1994).

17. See Ronald E. Clements, ed., *The World of Ancient Israel: Sociological, Anthropological, and Political Perspectives: Essays by Members of the Society of Old Testament Study* (Cambridge: Cambridge University Press, 1989).

18. Geert Hofstede, *Cultures and Organizations: Software of the Mind* (London: McGraw-Hill, 1991).

19. Victor H. Matthews, and Don C. Benjamin, *Social World of Ancient Israel: 1250–587 BCE* (Peabody, MA: Hendrickson, 1993).

20. Philip J. King and Lawrence E. Stager, *Life in Biblical Israel* (Louisville: Westminster John Knox, 2001).

21. Oded Borowski, *Daily Life in Biblical Times* (Atlanta: Society of Biblical Literature, 2003).

22. H. Wheeler Robinson, *Corporate Personality in Ancient Israel* (Philadelphia: Fortress, 1980).

23. Gary A. Anderson, *A Time to Mourn, A Time to Dance: The Expression of Grief and Joy in Israelite Religion* (University Park, PA: Pennsylvania State University, 1991).

24. Timothy Laniak, *Shepherds After My Own Heart: Pastoral Traditions and Leadership in the Bible* (Leicester, UK: Inter-Varsity, 2006).

25. Mary Douglas, *Purity and Danger: An Analysis of the Concepts of Pollution and Taboo* (New York: Routledge & Kegan Paul, 1966).

26. Edmund Leach, "The Logic of Sacrifice," *Anthropological Approaches to the Old Testament*, ed. Bernhard Lang (Philadelphia: Fortress, 1985).

27. Jacob Milgrom, *Leviticus, Anchor Bible Commentary*, 3 vols. (New York: Doubleday, 1991–2001).

28. Patrick D. Miller, *The Religion of Ancient Israel* (Louisville: Westminster John Knox, 2000).

29. James Maxwell Miller, *The Old Testament and the Historian* (Philadelphia: Fortress, 1976), 12–13.

30. John H. Walton, *Ancient Israelite Literature in its Cultural Context* (Grand Rapids: Zondervan, 1989).

31. Bruce Feiler, *Walking the Bible: A Journey by Land through the Five Books of Moses* (New York: Perennial, 2002).

32. Baruch Halpern, *David's Secret Demons: Messiah, Murderer, Traitor, King* (Grand Rapids: Eerdmans, 2001).

33. Hallo and Younger, ed., *Context of Scripture*.

34. See Clements, ed. *The World of Ancient Israel*; Robert P. Gordon and Johannes C. De Moor, eds., *The Old Testament in Its World* (Leiden: Brill, 2005); Alfred J. Hoerth et al., eds., *Peoples of the Old Testament World* (Grand Rapids: Baker, 1998); V. Philips Long, ed., *Israel's Past in Present Research: Essays on Ancient Israelite Historiography* (Winona Lake, IN: Eisenbrauns, 1999); Jack M. Sasson, ed., *Civilizations of the Ancient Near East*, 4 vols. (New York: Charles Scriber's Sons, 1995); Daniel C. Snell, *Life in the Ancient Near East: 3100–332 B.C.E.* (New Haven: Yale University Press, 1998); and Roland de Vaux, *Ancient Israel: Its Life and Institutions* (Grand Rapids: Eerdmans, 1997).

35. See Associates for Biblical Research at http://abr.christiananswers.net/home.html.

Chapter 9: Toward the Effective Preaching of New Testament Texts That Cite the Old Testament

1. It is a privilege to contribute this essay in honor of Walter C. Kaiser Jr., who has made such significant contributions to these areas. Anyone who has heard him preach knows that he provides wonderful examples of all of these uses of Scripture. His frequent playful suggestions of "marginal readings" remind one of the wonderful spirit found in so much rabbinic usage of Scripture. Such playful asides provide a touch of humor and endear him to his listeners as well as revealing the intimate ways in which the language and themes of Scripture saturate his heart and mind.

2. The functions of biblical quotations in the New Testament have been categorized in a variety of ways. Walter Kaiser has discussed the most important quotations of the Old Testament in the New under the categories of apologetic, prophetic, typological, theological, and practical uses in *The Uses of the Old Testament in the New* (Chicago: Moody, 1985). See pages 6–9 of his work for references to other classification systems.

3. Literacy and familiarity with written works were marks of the cultural elite. As Harry Gamble has pointed out, given "a community in which texts had a constitutive importance and only a few persons were literate, it was inevitable that those who were able to explicate texts would acquire authority for that reason alone" (Harry Y. Gamble, *Books and Readers in the Early Church: A History of Early Christian Texts* [New Haven: Yale University Press, 1995], 10, cited in Christopher D. Stanley, *Arguing with Scripture: The Rhetoric of Quotations in the Letters of Paul* [New York and London: T & T Clark, 2004], 46n25).

4. Herbert H. Clark and Richard R. Gerrig affirm this role in the use of some quotations: "When speakers demonstrate only a snippet of an event, they tacitly assume that their addressees share the right background to interpret it the same way they do.

In essence they are asserting, 'I am demonstrating something we both can interpret correctly,' and that implies solidarity" ("Quotations as Demonstrations," *Language* 66 (1990): 793; cited in Stanley, *Arguing with Scripture*, 32). G. B. Caird makes the same point in relation to the role of allusions in the New Testament: "Much of the use of the Old Testament in the New is of this allusive kind, establishing rapport between author and reader and giving confidence in a background of shared assumptions. A quotation may be the basis of an appeal to authority, but an allusion is always a reminder of what is held in common" (*The Language and Imagery of the Bible* [London: Duckworth Publishing, 1988], 33).

5. For example, Moisés Silva suggests that Paul uses the language of Deut. 19:15 in 2 Cor. 13:1 "to heighten the emotive thrust of his words" ("Old Testament in Paul," in the *Dictionary of Paul and His Letters*, ed. Gerald F. Hawthorne and Ralph P. Martin [Downers Grove, IL: InterVarsity, 1993], 638). Richard Hays suggests Paul echoes Job 13:16 LXX in Phil. 1:19 ("this will turn out for my deliverance") and thereby "tacitly likens himself to Job" and in doing so "whispers a suggestion that the rival preachers have assumed the mantle of Job's hollow comforters" (*Echoes of Scripture in the Letters of Paul* [New Haven and London: Yale University Press, 1989], 23). Hays suggests "Paul's citations of Scripture often function not as proofs but as tropes: they generate new meanings by linking the earlier text (Scripture) to the later (Paul's discourse) in such a way as to produce unexpected correspondences, correspondences that suggest more than they assert" (*Echoes*, 24).

6. The "aha" suggests that the authors actually understood all the insights in their writings, while many people seem to hold an implicit view of inspiration that leaves some doubt regarding whether or not the authors really understood what they were writing even as they wrote it.

7. This is an anachronistic description, of course, since the Bereans would not all have had their own personal copies of the Bible. There would have been very few copies of the Scriptures (possibly only one copy or possibly only copies of certain books) for the whole church. See the discussion of Stanley, *Arguing with Scripture*, 41–43. Stanley provides an important reminder that most of the members of Paul's churches would not be literate and would not have ready access to biblical scrolls. He does not grapple with the implications of Luke's description in Acts 17:11. Luke does not tell us *how* that study of the Scriptures took place; how much of the Scripture they had access to (less than the whole Old Testament Canon or multiple copies of the Canon); how many members were literate vs. the number of illiterate members; whether the literate members of the congregation read the appropriate Old Testament texts out loud to the rest of the congregation so that they could discuss them. While I consider Luke to be an accurate and inspired author (and would date the book to sometime between AD 66–85), even scholars who date the book of Acts later than others and those who doubt Luke's historical accuracy on other issues must deal with the fact that Luke expects his description to sound realistic and to pass the "laugh test" with his readers as a description of a mid-first-century situation. Thus even critical scholars should weigh Luke's description more seriously when considering the possible knowledge of Scripture among Paul's readers. For a scholar to think Luke might be mistaken is one thing; to think that he would be rhetorically foolish enough to provide his first-century readers with descriptions of social situations that do not plausibly reflect reality is itself not really plausible. Two other points should be made. Luke is describing the readership of a first-century synagogue while Paul writes to churches. But those churches were likely to reflect the readership of the ancient synagogue since its members were prob-

ably drawn from that context to begin with (see Acts 17:12). Also, that Luke describes the Bereans' behavior as marking them out as "more noble" than the Thessalonians suggests that in his view the Thessalonians (and others) could have done the same as the Bereans (it is not that the latter, by some strange circumstance, had easier access to the study of the Scriptures than the former).

8. Some of the different ways in which New Testament authors reflect the influence of Scripture in their thinking and arguments include quotations with or without introductory formulae (such as "as it is written"); allusions to Old Testament texts; echoes of scriptural texts; interpretive summaries (1 Corinthians 15; Luke 24); general references to the Scriptures or to the Law; presupposition or implied understanding of Old Testament background, motifs, or teaching; and the influence of Old Testament (especially septuagintal) style and diction.

9. Another way of describing the situation would be to say that the New Testament authors are like gifted jazz musicians whose music is evaluated by people who are only familiar with classical music and who evaluate that music not on its own terms but as failing to meet the standards and expectations that they have for fine (classical) music.

10. See the articles dealing with this issue from various perspectives in G. K. Beale, ed., *The Right Doctrine from the Wrong Texts? Essays on the Use of the Old Testament in the New* (Grand Rapids: Baker, 1994).

11. Moisés Silva makes a similar point with reference to the "greatly compressed" nature of rabbinic biblical quotations and interpretations: "Two or three words might call to mind a whole passage of Scripture, plus other parallel passages, plus a body of tradition that linked those passages with the point being made. Similarly, our inability to identify all the logical steps that might have led Paul to use an Old Testament text for a particular purpose may reflect nothing more than our ignorance" ("Old Testament in Paul," 639).

12. Some obvious examples include Mark 12:26 (where the point depends upon the tense of the verb [implied in the Hebrew and in Mark's text but supplied in the LXX); Gal. 3:16 (where the argument depends upon the number [plural] of the noun); Rom. 4:10–11 (where the argument depends upon the context of Gen. 15:6).

13. This difference between ancient and modern interpretation is also reflected in the fact that we tend to specialize in the interpretation of discrete individual texts while ancient and biblical authors frequently provide interpretations (and applications) of huge swaths of texts in one extended passage. Thus the author of the letter to the Hebrews interprets much of the Old Testament as a history of the acts of people of faith (chap. 11), and Stephen interprets much of Old Testament history as one marked by the intransigence of God's people (Acts 7). Paul can summarize the history of redemption in terms of the actions of the first and last Adams and the reigns introduced by each (Rom. 5:12–21). Already in the Old Testament certain psalms provided interpretive overviews of Israel's history (Psalms 78, 105, 106, 114, 135, 136) and other legal and prophetic passages also provided summarizing overviews of biblical history. These and other reinterpretations of Israel's history or of biblical texts are referred to by scholars as "rewritten Bible" and are found in the Old Testament as well as in ancient Jewish and New Testament texts. The most extensive canonical example of "rewritten Bible" is found in 1–2 Chronicles, which retell much of the material in 1–2 Samuel and 1–2 Kings in such a way as to bring out the relevance of God's past work and promises for the situation of the post-exilic community. Extensive noncanonical examples are

found in *Jubilees*, the *Genesis Apocryphon* (1Qap Genar), Josephus's *Antiquities*, and many other ancient Jewish writings.

14. The second most common rabbinic method of interpretation found in the New Testament is called *qal wahomer* (light and heavy), and entails the use of a fortiori argumentation—the argument that what applies in a lesser case most certainly applies in a weightier case (1 Cor. 9:8–12; Heb. 9:13–14; 10:28–29).

15. In Hebrew both texts have *w'ahavta* while in the LXX they both have *kai agapēseis*.

16. In Hebrew the verb is *hashav* while in Greek it is *logizomai*.

17. In Rom. 15:9–12 Paul ties together a series of texts dealing with the joy and blessing of the "Gentiles," while in 1 Peter 2:6–8, Peter ties together a series of passages dealing with attitudes regarding destiny-determining "stones."

18. See Walter C. Kaiser Jr., *Toward an Exegetical Theology* (Grand Rapids: Baker, 1981), 131–40.

19. Kaiser, *The Uses of the Old Testament in the New*, 69.

20. Kaiser, *Toward an Exegetical Theology*, 136.

21. Kaiser, *The Uses of the Old Testament in the New*, 69.

22. Kaiser, *Toward an Exegetical Theology*, 137.

23. See the lists of presuppositions provided by G. K. Beale, "Did Jesus and His Followers Preach the Right Doctrine from the Wrong Texts?" in Beale, *The Right Doctrine from the Wrong Texts?*, 392, and by Klyne Snodgrass, "The Use of the Old Testament in the New," in Beale, *The Right Doctrine from the Wrong Texts?*, 36–40.

24. The most obvious texts are the references to the "servant" in Isaiah who is explicitly identified with Israel/Jacob in some places but seems to refer to an individual who redeems and restores Israel in others (cf. Isa. 41:8–9; 42:1, 19; 43:10; 44:1–2, 21; 45:4; 48:20; 49:3–7; 50:10; 52:13; 53:11), and the "one like a son of man" in Daniel 7 who appears to be an individual regent in verse 13 but is later interpreted to be a reference to "the saints of the Most High" (vv. 18–27). See the discussion of this presupposition provided by Snodgrass, "The Use of the Old Testament in the New," in Beale, *The Right Doctrine from the Wrong Texts?*, 37. This idea is reflected in N. T. Wright's observation that what Paul "had expected God to do for Israel at the end of all things, God had done for Jesus in the middle of all things. In and through Jesus Israel's hope had been realized. He had been raised from the dead, after suffering and dying at the hands of the pagans" (*What Saint Paul Really Said: Was Paul of Tarsus the Real Founder of Christianity?* [Grand Rapids: Eerdmans, 1997], 127).

25. Snodgrass, "The Use of the Old Testament in the New," in Beale, *The Right Doctrine from the Wrong Texts?*, 38. This is usually referred to as "typology," on which see David W. Baker, "Typology and the Christian Use of the Old Testament," in Beale, *The Right Doctrine from the Wrong Texts?*, 313–30; G. P. Hugenberger, "Introductory Notes on Typology," in Beale, *The Right Doctrine from the Wrong Texts?*, 331–41; Francis Foulkes, "The Acts of God: A Study of the Basis of Typology in the Old Testament," in Beale, *The Right Doctrine from the Wrong Texts?*, 342–71; Richard M. Davidson, *Typology in Scripture: A Study of Hermeneutical TUPOS Structures* (Berrien Springs, MI: Andrews University Press, 1981); L. Goppelt, *Typos: The Typological Interpretation of the Old Testament in the New* (Grand Rapids: Eerdmans, 1982). Elsewhere I have suggested that in Paul's usage Scripture frequently serves as a "tool for redescription" by which readers' perceptions of their own situations and the appropriate response within their situation is guided by redescribing them in terms of Old Testament parallels. Such redescription is governed by the broader theological and hermeneutical

structure that dictates which are the most appropriate parallels to the new situation faced by the believers. While anything can be described in any way, the New Testament use of the Old Testament suggests that not all redescriptions are equally valid and it is of utmost importance to interpret the situations we face according to the most appropriate biblical analogy. See Roy E. Ciampa, *The Presence and Function of Scripture in Galatians 1 and 2*, Wissenschaftliche Untersuchungen zum Neuen Testament 2.102 (Tübingen: J. C. B. Mohr Siebeck, 1998), 227–32.

26. Most studies have tended to focus on the Christological orientation of the use of the Old Testament in the New (see Donald H. Juel, *Messianic Exegesis: Christological Interpretation of the Old Testament in Early Christianity* [Philadelphia: Fortress, 1988]; N. T. Wright, *The Climax of the Covenant: Christ and the Law in Pauline Theology* [Edinburgh: T & T Clark, 1991]). Richard B. Hays has stressed the ecclesiological orientation of much of Paul's interpretation of the Old Testament (*Echoes of Scripture in the Letters of Paul*; cf. Hans K. LaRondelle, *The Israel of God in Prophecy: Principles of Prophetic Interpretation* [Berrien Springs, MI: Andrews University Press, 1983]); Dietrich-Alex Koch (*Die Schrift als Zeuge des Evangeliums: Untersuchungen zur Verwendung und zum Verständnis der Schrift bei Paulus*, Beiträge zur historischen Theologie 69 [Tübingen: J. C. B. Mohr Siebeck, 1986]) has stressed Paul's understanding of "Scripture as a witness to the gospel."

27. One example of this is found in the New Testament's use of the language of "inheritance," which in the Old Testament usually focused on inheriting the Promised Land while in the New Testament it is not the Land that God's people hope to inherit but the "earth" or "world" (Matt. 5:5; Rom. 4:13), or "the kingdom of God" (Matt. 25:34; 1 Cor. 6:9–10; 15:50; Gal. 4:30; 5:21; Eph. 5:5; Col. 1:12; James 2:5; 1 Peter 1:4), or "eternal life" (Matt. 19:29; Mark 10:17; Luke 10:25; 18:18).

28. In Greek, quotations were sometimes introduced with *hoti* (Matt. 7:23) and other times with a neuter article (Matt. 19:18), but those both served other purposes as well, and many quotations were not introduced with either. Biblical authors sometimes used quotation formulas such as "it is written" (Matt. 4:4), but most quotations are not introduced with such a formula.

29. See Christopher D. Stanley, *Paul and the Language of Scripture: Citation Technique in the Pauline Epistles and Contemporary Literature*, Society for New Testament Studies Monograph Series, 69 (Cambridge: Cambridge University Press, 1992), 267–337, for discussion of the accepted citation practices in the context of the New Testament.

30. Evidence suggests that revisions of the LXX which brought it closer to the text we now find in the Masoretic Text (MT) were already in existence at the time of the New Testament so that even when a quotation agrees with the MT against the LXX, we cannot be certain that the person was quoting from Hebrew. They may have been quoting from a Greek text that agreed more closely to the Hebrew of the MT than the LXX.

31. See the essays on both sides of this issue in Beale, *The Right Doctrine from the Wrong Texts?*

32. C. H. Dodd, "The Old Testament in the New," in Beale, *The Right Doctrine from the Wrong Texts?*, 176. His fuller defense of this view can be found in C. H. Dodd, *According to the Scriptures: The Sub-structure of New Testament Theology* (London: Fontana, 1952).

33. Other people who supposed themselves to be prophets had also associated themselves with a ministry in the wilderness, presumably in light of texts like Isaiah 40:3. See Josephus, *Jewish Antiquities* 20:167, 188; *The Jewish War* 2:259–62.

34. Repentance in the form of an intentional alignment with God's commands is what Isaiah has in mind and is what Deuteronomy 30:1–6 called for as a prerequisite for restoration from exile and the other covenantal curses.

35. Another example in Matthew is found in the way Mary's conception is referred to in 1:18, as (literally) "to have in the womb" (*en gastri echousa*). There are a variety of ways in which conception may be referred to, and this is not the most common one (Matt. 1:20 uses the verb *gennan* ["to procreate, beget"]; Luke uses the verb *syllambanein* ["to conceive, become pregnant"; 1:24, 31; 2:21]). Matthew's description of Mary is tailored to the wording of the Old Testament text he is about to cite so that his understanding of her relation to it might be perfectly clear. Matthew does the same in his lead-up to his quotation from Isaiah 9:1–2 in 4:15–16. In verse 13 he tells us Jesus "went and lived in Capernaum by the sea, in the territory of Zebulun and Naphtali." It is unlikely that people in Matthew's day normally identified Capernaum by the fact that it was in the ancient territory of Zebulun and Naphtali. But the quote from Isaiah identifies the place where Isaiah's prophecy would be fulfilled by reference to the land of Zebulun and the land of Naphtali. If Matthew had simply said that Jesus had moved to Capernaum the reader may have missed the tie-in to the Scripture quotation.

36. The noun *euangelion* in Mark 1:1 is based on the verb *euangelizein* which is found twice in Isaiah 40:9 (cf. Isa. 52:7; 61:1).

37. Sometimes the argument of a New Testament author has been based on scriptural texts long before he gets around to citing them (or even when he never gets around to citing them!). For example, Paul quotes both Gen. 15:6 (Abram "believed the LORD, and he counted it to him as righteousness") and Habakkuk 2:4 ("the righteous will live by his faith") in Galatians 3 (vv. 6, 11). But long before he gets to that, his discussion of justification by faith in 2:16 is based on those same texts (see Roy E. Ciampa, *The Presence and Function of Scripture in Galatians 1 and 2*, 191–97).

38. As Silva ("Old Testament in Paul," 638) puts it, "Paul's use of the Old Testament was not motivated by antiquarian interests. The Scriptures were intensely practical for him. . . . It is precisely because Paul is never content with merely restating the original, historical meaning of an Old Testament text, but rather applies it to his present situation, that the perennial and troublesome question arises, 'Can we use Paul's exegesis today?' The very formulation of the problem can be misleading. Usually what is in view is whether Paul's methods of interpretation are compatible with 'scientific,' grammatico-historical exegesis. But this concern often ignores some fundamental obstacles. In the first place, Paul never gives us an exegetical discussion in the usual sense. . . . To put it differently: there is no evidence that Paul or his contemporaries ever sat down to 'exegete' Old Testament texts in a way comparable to what today's seminary students are expected to do—that is, to produce an exposition that focuses on the historical meaning. Nevertheless, many of Paul's actual uses of Scripture are acknowledged by all concerned to be consistent with such a historical meaning. In other words, there is plenty of evidence that the apostle reflected carefully and thoughtfully on Old Testament texts in their contexts. Even in the case of quotations that appear somewhat arbitrary, patient consideration of the broad context can be enlightening."

39. Rikki Watts, *Isaiah's New Exodus in Mark* (Grand Rapids: Baker, 2000), 370. He sees the three main sections of Mark's Gospel following the structure of "Isaiah's New Exodus schema" where Yahweh first delivers Israel from "the power of the na-

tions and their idols," then leads them along the "way of the Lord," and finally makes a triumphal entry with them into Jerusalem (123–36).

40. See N. T. Wright's understanding of the biblical interpretation implied in Romans 1:1–5 (N. T. Wright, "Romans," in *The New Interpreter's Bible*, vol. 12 [Nashville: Abingdon, 2002]) and C. E. B. Cranfield's view that Habakkuk 2:4, which Paul quotes in Romans 1:17, provides the structure for the first eight chapters of that letter (C. E. B. Cranfield, *Romans: A Shorter Commentary* [Grand Rapids: Eerdmans, 1985, xv]). Also Todd A. Wilson, "Wilderness Apostasy and Paul's Portrayal of the Crisis in Galatians," *New Testament Studies* 50 (2004): 550–71, suggests Paul's echo of Israel's wilderness apostasy in the opening verses of the letter, along with other echoes of the same, set the tone for the letter as a whole. For a helpful discussion of the role of the prologue of Galatians in the letter as a whole see D. Cook, "The Prescript as Programme in Galatians," *Journal of Theological Studies* 43ns (1992): 511–19. For the place of the opening of 1 Corinthians in the structure of the letter as a whole, see Roy E. Ciampa and Brian S. Rosner in the forthcoming "The Structure and Argument of 1 Corinthians: A Biblical/Jewish Approach," *New Testament Studies* 52 (2006).

41. This is another (subtle) example of "rewritten Bible." Although Cyrus's decree played a significant role in the history of Israel, giving the Jews permission to return to their own land, it is not mentioned by Matthew, whose implied and explicit interpretations of Scripture suggest that for him Israel's exilic status has continued, in some sense, right up to the coming of Christ. This understanding was not unique to Matthew, but rather was fairly common among certain groups of Jews in the intertestamental period. See O. H. Steck, "Das Problem theologischer Strömungen in nachexilischer Zeit," *Evangelische Theologie* 28 (1968): 445–581; Michael A. Knibb, "The Exile in the Literature of the Intertestamental Period," *Heythrop Journal* 17 (1976): 253–72; George W. E. Nickelsburg, *Jewish Literature Between the Bible and the Mishnah: A Historical and Literary Introduction*, 2nd ed. (Minneapolis: Fortress, 2005), 18; Jacob Neusner, *Self-Fulfilling Prophecy: Exile and Restoration in the History of Israel* (Boston: Beacon, 1987), 58–60; James M. Scott, "'For as Many as are of Works of the Law are under a Curse' (Galatians 3.10)," in *Paul and the Scriptures of Israel*, ed. Craig A. Evans and James A. Sanders, Journal for the Study of the New Testament: Supplement Series 83; *Studies in Early Judaism and Christianity* 1 (Sheffield: Sheffield Academic Press, 1993), 194–213; idem, "Paul's Use of Deuteronomic Tradition," *Journal of Biblical Literature* 112 (1993): 645–65; idem, "Jesus' Vision for the Restoration of Israel as the Basis for a Biblical Theology of the New Testament," in *Biblical Theology: Retrospect and Prospect*, ed. Scott J. Hafemann (Downers Grove, IL: InterVarsity, 2002), 129–43; idem, "Restoration of Israel," in *The Dictionary of Paul and His Letters*, ed. Hawthorne and Martin, 796–805; Wright, *The New Testament and the People of God*, 268–72 (see the literature cited on his page 270n108); C. Marvin Pate, J. Scott Duvall, J. Daniel Hayes, E. Randolph Richards, W. Dennis Tucker Jr., and Preben Vang, *The Story of Israel: A Biblical Theology* (Downers Grove, IL: InterVarsity, 2004). This view has been contested (cf. I. H. Jones, "Disputed Questions in Biblical Studies: 4. Exile and Eschatology," *Expository Times* 112 (2000–2001): 401–5; M. Casey, "Where Wright is Wrong," *Journal for the Study of the New Testament* 69 (1998): 95–103; Mark A. Seifrid, "Blind Alleys in the Controversy over the Paul of History," *Tyndale Bulletin* 45 (1994): 73–95; James D. G. Dunn, *Jesus Remembered*, Christianity in the Making, 1 (Grand Rapids: Eerdmans, 2003), 473 and note 422; Steven M. Bryan, *Jesus and Israel's Traditions of Judgement and Restoration*, Society for New Testament Studies Monograph Series, 117 (Cambridge: Cambridge University Press, 2002), 12–20. See the responses in Scott J. Hafemann,

"Paul and the Exile of Israel in Galatians 3–4" in *Exile: Old Testament, Jewish, and Christian Conceptions*, ed. James M. Scott (Leiden: Brill, 1997), 368–69n74; Steven G. Dempster, *Dominion and Dynasty: A Biblical Theology of the Hebrew Bible*, New Studies in Biblical Theology, 15 (Downers Grove, IL: InterVarsity, 2003), 219n7.

42. Evidence for such ancient exegeses can be found not only in the New Testament but also in ancient Jewish literature such as the Dead Sea Scrolls, the Old Testament Apocrypha, the Old Testament Pseudepigrapha, the writings of Philo and Josephus (cf. Martin Jan Mulder, ed., *Mikra: Text, Translation, Reading and Interpretation of the Hebrew Bible in Ancient Judaism and Early Christianity*, Compendia rerum iudaicarum ad Novum Testamentum, 2.1 [Assen & Maastricht: Van Gorcum; Minneapolis: Fortress, 1990]). Rabbinic literature, while coming from a later period than the New Testament, has many traditions going back to the New Testament period. On the latter see David Instone-Brewer, *Traditions of the Rabbis from the Era of the New Testament* (Grand Rapids: Eerdmans, 2004).

43. See Douglas J. Moo, *The Epistle to the Romans*, New International Commentary on the New Testament (Grand Rapids: Eerdmans, 1996), 256.

44. For helpful guidance on these questions see D. A. Carson and G. K. Beale, eds., *Commentary on the Use of the Old Testament in the New* (Grand Rapids: Baker, forthcoming).

Chapter 10: Preaching the Old Testament Today

1. The biblical preacher must preach from Old Testament texts regularly and rigorously. No one in our times has so relentlessly called us to this demanding task as has Walter C. Kaiser Jr. He has been without peer in sounding this message in both classroom and conference ministry around the world. What is more, he has passionately embodied his burden in his own volcanic preaching. Kaiser's love for the text is legendary and it is a high honor for me to make a small contribution toward more serious preaching of the Old Testament in tribute to Kaiser and in grateful praise to our God.

2. Ray Lubeck, *Read the Bible for a Change: A Follower's Guide to Reading and Responding to the Bible* (Waynesboro, GA: Authentic Media, 2005), 14.

Chapter 11: Preaching the Old Testament Evangelistically

1. "The Laws, Liberties and Orders of Harvard College, Confirmed by the Overseers and President of the College in the years 1642, 1643, 1644, 1645, and 1646, and Published by the Scholars for the Perpetual Preservation of their Welfare and Government," cited by Josiah Quincy, *The History of Harvard University*, vol. 1 (Boston: Crosby, Nichols, Lee & Co., 1860), 515.

2. The word *disciple* (*mathētēs*) describes a learner, as in the sense of an apprentice or student. Though the term can be applied to any master-pupil relationship, as used in the Gospels it usually denotes those persons who follow Christ, and "always implies the existence of a personal attachment which shapes the whole life of the one described." *Theological Dictionary of the New Testament*, vol. 4, ed. Gerhard Kittel, trans. and ed. Geoffrey W. Bromiley (Grand Rapids: Eerdmans, 1967), 441.

3. The Lausanne Covenant, Article 3.

4. I draw heavily here on my presentation, "Focusing the Message," in *Choose Ye This Day* (Minneapolis: World Wide Publications, 1989), 65–77. Also, Robert Coleman, "An Evangelistic Sermon Checklist," *Christianity Today* (November 5, 1969): 27–28.

5. Charles Haddon Spurgeon, "Lectures to My Students," cited in Sidney Greidanus, *Preaching Christ from the Old Testament* (Grand Rapids: Eerdmans, 1999), 2.

6. No one has expressed this unity of the Scriptures more profoundly, yet simply, than Walter C. Kaiser Jr., in his lectures published under the title, *The Christian and the "Old" Testament* (Pasadena: William Carey Library, 1998). One wanting to get an invigorating sweep of biblical theology as related to this subject would do well to begin with this book.

7. Greidanus, *Preaching Christ from the Old Testament*, 227–350.

8. Tracing this theme through the Old Testament is a fascinating study. Among the many authors who have thought long on this subject are Walter C. Kaiser Jr., *The Messiah of the Old Testament* (Grand Rapids: Zondervan, 1995); Wilhelm Vischer, *The Witness of the Old Testament to Christ*, trans. A. B. Crabtree (London: Lutterworth Press, 1949); Alfred Edersheim, *Prophecy and History in Relation to the Messiah* (New York: Anson D. F. Randolf, 1885); Charles Augustus Briggs, *Messianic Prophecy* (New York: Charles Scribner's Sons, 1889); and E. W. Hengstenberg's monumental four-volume work, *Christology of the Old Testament and a Commentary on the Messianic Predictions* (Grand Rapids: Kregel, 1956, 1972–1978).

9. For a comprehensive treatment of this theme through the Bible, see Robert E. Coleman, *The New Covenant* (Deerfield, IL: Christian Outreach, 1992, 1984).

10. This story is recounted in Coleman, *The New Covenant*, 12–13.

11. This kingdom motif has received considerable attention from biblical scholars, resulting in a plethora of literature. A comprehensive and readable study of its historical development, particularly in the Old Testament, is John Bright's *The Kingdom of God* (New York: Abingdon-Cokesbury, 1953). An evangelical writer in this area who deserves special attention is George Eldon Ladd, especially his *Crucial Questions About the Kingdom of God* (Grand Rapids: Eerdmans, 1968, 1952) and his *Jesus and the Kingdom* (New York: Harper & Row, 1964).

12. Any good textbook in homiletics will address this issue though few develop it in depth. Among those particularly concerned with evangelistic preaching are books by David Larsen, *The Evangelistic Mandate* (Grand Rapids: Kregel, 1992); Ramesh Richard, *Preaching Evangelistic Sermons* (Grand Rapids: Baker, 2005); and Lloyd M. Perry and John R. Strubhar, *Evangelistic Preaching* (Chicago: Moody, 1979).

13. Taking this idea to the extreme, an innovative view of evangelistic preaching that centers on the community instead of the preaching is put forth by Priscilla Pope-Levison and John R. Levison, "Evangelistic Preaching in the New Millennium," *The Journal of the Academy for Evangelism in Theological Education*, vol. 19 (2003–2004): 84–91.

14. One wanting to pursue this area of preparation will find helpful works of R. Alan Street, *The Effective Invitation* (Old Tappan, NJ: Revell, 1984); Roy J. Fish, *Giving a Good Invitation* (Nashville: Broadman, 1974); Faris D. Whitesell, *Sixty-five Ways to Give Evangelistic Invitations* (Grand Rapids: Zondervan, 1945); and shorter treatments in Ramesh Richard, *Preaching Evangelistic Sermons*, Chapter 10 and Appendix 5; also Leighton Ford, "The Place of Decision," *Choose Ye This Day*, 87–108.

15. An excellent treatment of most of the major Old Testament revivals is by Walter C. Kaiser Jr., *Revive Us Again: Your Wake-up Call for Spiritual Revival* (Ross-Shire, Scotland: Christian Focus Publications, 2001). To this could be added the work of C. E. Aubrey, *Revivals of the Old Testament* (Grand Rapids: Zondervan, 1960); and from both Testaments, the older work of Ernest Baker, *Great Revivals of the Bible* (London: The Kingsgate, 1906).

16. Most of the sermons recorded in the book of Acts have an evangelistic ring, and, as we would expect, they draw upon the Bible of their day, the Old Testament. See especially the messages recorded in Acts 4:8–12; 5:29–32; 7:1–53; 10:34–48; and 13:16–41.

17. Told by F. W. Boreham, *A Late Lark Singing* (London: Epworth Press, 1945), 66.

18. Josiah Quincy, *History of Harvard University*, 515.

Afterword: Preaching the Old Testament

1. Kaiser, *Toward an Exegetical Theology*, 8.

Contributors

Jeffrey D. Arthurs is Associate Professor of Preaching and Dean of the Chapel at Gordon-Conwell Theological Seminary, South Hamilton, Massachusetts. He earned the Bachelor of Arts (B.A.) and the Master of Arts (M.A.) at Bob Jones University, the Master of Arts (M.A.) at Western Seminary, and the Doctor of Philosophy (Ph.D.) at Purdue University.

Roy E. Ciampa is Director of the Th.M. program in Biblical Studies and Associate Professor of New Testament at Gordon-Conwell Theological Seminary, South Hamilton, Massachusetts. He earned the Bachelor of Arts (B.A.) at Gordon College, the Master of Divinity (M.Div.) at Denver Seminary, and the Doctor of Philosophy (Ph.D.) at the University of Aberdeen, Scotland.

Robert E. Coleman is Distinguished Professor of Discipleship and Evangelism at Gordon-Conwell Theological Seminary, South Hamilton, Massachusetts. He earned the Bachelor of Divinity (B.D.) at Asbury Theological Seminary, a Master of Theology (M.Th.) at Princeton Theological Seminary, the Doctor of Philosophy (Ph.D.) at the University of Iowa, and the Doctor of Divinity (D.D.) from Trinity International University.

Duane A. Garrett is Professor of Old Testament Interpretation at Southern Baptist Theological Seminary, Louisville, Kentucky. He earned the Master of Divinity (M.Div.) at Trinity Evangelical Divinity School and the Doctor of Philosophy (Ph.D.) at Baylor University.

Scott M. Gibson is the Haddon W. Robinson Professor of Preaching and Ministry and Director of the Center for Preaching at Gordon-Conwell Theological Seminary, South Hamilton, Massachusetts, where he teaches homiletics. He earned the Master of Divinity (M.Div.) at Gordon-Conwell Theological Seminary, the Master of Theology (Th.M.) at Princeton Theological Seminary in homiletics, the Master of Theology (M.Th.) in church history from the University of Toronto, and the Doctor of Philosophy (D.Phil.) degree from the University of Oxford. He was a pastor in Pennsylvania before coming to teach at the seminary.

Carol M. Kaminski is Assistant Professor of Old Testament at Gordon-Conwell Theological Seminary, South Hamilton, Massachusetts. She earned the Master of Arts (M.A.) from Gordon-Conwell Theological Seminary and the Doctor of Philosophy (Ph.D.) from the University of Cambridge. A native of Australia, she served her local church in a ministry living with homeless young women, and before commencing her doctoral studies in England, she taught at the Bible College of Victoria.

Timothy S. Laniak is Assistant Professor of Old Testament at Gordon-Conwell Theological Seminary, Charlotte, North Carolina. He earned the Master of Divinity (M.Div.) from Gordon-Conwell Theological Seminary, engaged in doctoral studies at Brandeis University, and was awarded the Doctor of Theology (Th.D.) from Harvard Divinity School. In addition to a full schedule of teaching in churches, he has taught in schools in Japan and the Philippines. He directed a community house for international scholars and students in the Boston area and has consulted on international student ministry with Christian leaders in India, Nepal, Malaysia, Singapore, Thailand, Hong Kong, China, and Japan.

David L. Larsen is Professor Emeritus of Preaching at Trinity Evangelical Divinity School, Deerfield, Illinois. He holds the Master of Divinity (M.Div.) from Fuller Theological Seminary and the Doctor of Divinity (D.D.) from Trinity College. Before his retirement in 1996, he was chair of the department of practical theology and professor of practical theology at Trinity, where he served for fifteen years. Dr. Larsen pastored eight churches in North Dakota, Minnesota, California, and Illinois. He also served as visiting professor at Friendship Bible Institute in San Francisco, Simpson Bible College in San Francisco, and Rockford College in Rockford, Illinois.

Dennis R. Magary is Associate Professor of Old Testament and Semitic Languages at Trinity Evangelical Divinity School, Deerfield, Illinois. He earned the Master of Divinity (M.Div.) from Trinity Evangelical Divinity School and the Master of Arts (M.A.) and the Doctor of Philosophy (Ph.D.) in Hebrew and Semitic studies from the University of Wisconsin at Madison. Dr. Magary's areas of expertise include Hebrew, Old Testament, and computer applications for Old Testament studies.

Haddon W. Robinson is the Harold John Ockenga Distinguished Professor of Preaching at Gordon-Conwell Theological Seminary, South Hamilton, Massachusetts. He earned the Master of Theology (Th.M.) from Dallas Theological Seminary and the Master of Arts (M.A.) and the Doctor of Philosophy (Ph.D.) degrees in communication from Southern Methodist University and the University of Illinois, respectively.

John H. Sailhamer is Senior Professor of Old Testament and Hebrew at Southeastern Baptist Theological Seminary, Wake Forest, North Carolina. He earned the Master of Theology (Th.M.) at Dallas Theological Seminary and the Master of Arts (M.A.) and the Doctor of Philosophy (Ph.D.) from the University of Southern California at Los Angeles.

Douglas K. Stuart is Professor of Old Testament at Gordon-Conwell Theological Seminary, South Hamilton, Massachusetts. He received the Bachelor of Arts (B.A.) magna cum laude from Harvard College and spent two years in graduate study at Yale Divinity School. He earned the Doctor of Philosophy (Ph.D.) from Harvard University, where the subject of his thesis was Old Testament and early Semitic poetry.